THE EVERYTHING® Spanish Grammar Book

Dear Reader,

I started learning my first foreign language, English, in grade school and it soon became one of my favorite classes. I liked the concept of communicating in a different language, and memorization came easily to me.

However, once I found myself in the United States, acquiring fluency in English proved to be more challenging. Some of the grammar didn't make sense, and I had trouble understanding American pronunciation.

I can't tell you exactly when I realized that I'd finally made English my own, but I do know that I couldn't have done it without studying English grammar. I needed to learn the basics that come naturally to native speakers of English.

This is why I consider Spanish grammar a very important part of learning Spanish. Whether you're a non-native speaker and need to figure out concepts like the subjunctive mood and the multiple past tenses or a native speaker who never had the opportunity to study Spanish in a classroom setting, learning Spanish grammar can truly help you gain full proficiency in this beautiful language.

Julie Gutin

The EVERYTHING Series

Editorial

Publishing Director	Gary M. Krebs
Managing Editor	Kate McBride
Copy Chief	Laura M. Daly
Acquisitions Editors	Eric M. Hall / Gina Chaimanis
Development Editor	Katie McDonough
Language Editor	Susana Schultz
Production Editor	Jamie Wielgus

Production

Production Director	Susan Beale
Production Manager	Michelle Roy Kelly
Series Designers	Daria Perreault Colleen Cunningham
Cover Design	Paul Beatrice Matt Leblanc
Layout and Graphics	Colleen Cunningham Rachael Eiben Michelle Roy Kelly John Paulhus Daria Perreault Erin Ring
Series Cover Artist	Barry Littmann

THE EVERYTHING® SPANISH GRAMMAR BOOK

All the rules you need to master español

Julie Gutin

Adams Media
Avon, Massachusetts

To my parents, who made it all possible

Published by Adams Media, an F+W Publications Company
57 Littlefield Street, Avon, MA 02322 U.S.A.
www.adamsmedia.com

ISBN: 1-59337-309-0
Printed in Canada.

J I H G F E D C B A

Library of Congress Cataloging-in-Publication Data
Gutin, Julie.
The everything Spanish grammar book / Julie Gutin.
p. cm.
ISBN 1-59337-309-0
1. Spanish language–Grammar. 2. Spanish language–Textbooks for foreign speakers–English. I. Title. II. Series: Everything series.

PC4112.G87 2005
468.2'421–dc22

2004026355

Contents

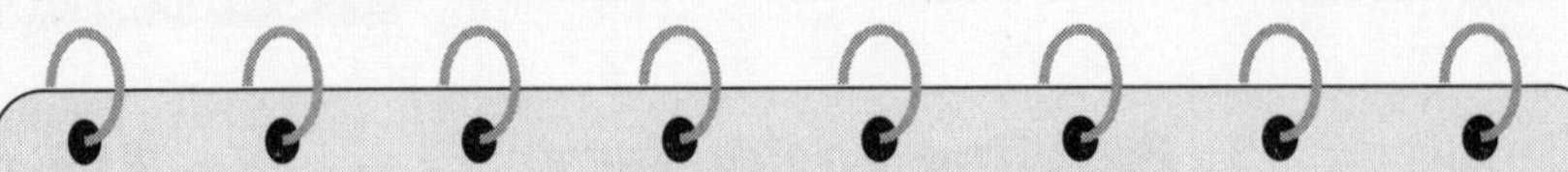

Top Ten Reasons *to Study Spanish Grammar*

1. It'll help you speak Spanish and be able to understand the responses.
2. It'll improve your reading comprehension so that you can finally get started on *Don Quixote*.
3. You'll never be stumped by verb conjugations again.
4. You'll finally figure out the purpose of the subjunctive mood and how to use it correctly.
5. You can finally stop embarrassing yourself by addressing your teacher with the informal "you," *tú*.
6. It will help you improve your English grammar skills.
7. You'll be a lot more sympathetic to those who are learning English and are struggling with it.
8. You can impress native Spanish speakers with your knowledge of Spanish grammar.
9. You'll learn why native Spanish speakers make certain mistakes when using English grammar.
10. You can figure it all out, once and for all, and then finally be able to move on to all the fun stuff, like traveling abroad.

Acknowledgments

I would like to thank my family—Nonna, Faina, and Leonid Gutin—for all their love and support. To Veronica, thanks for listening and for keeping me company when I couldn't stand working anymore. And to ShihYan—thanks for being there.

This project couldn't have happened without Eric Hall, my acquisitions editor, who believed in me and gave me the freedom to make this project what I wanted it to be. And I owe special thanks to Kate McBride, who supported me in this undertaking. A lot of credit for this book also goes to Gina Chaimanis, who masterfully took over this project, and to the rest of the Adams team—Gary Krebs, Laura MacLaughlin, Jamie Wielgus, the production department (Michelle Roy Kelly, thanks for a great layout!), and of course fellow development editors, Karen Jacot and Christina MacDonald.

Finally, I would like to acknowledge all of my Spanish teachers—your hard work made this book possible. I couldn't have done it without you!

Introduction

SOME PEOPLE REALLY ENJOY STUDYING GRAMMAR, but for most of us, grammar is nothing more than a special torture devised by bored teachers who wish to break down a language into a myriad little rules that must all be followed without question. But is it really all that bad?

Linguists say that there are actually two types of grammar—prescriptive and descriptive. Prescriptive grammar is a collection of rules about how a language *should* behave. Inflexible rules that the grade school teachers have instilled in us—never end a sentence with a preposition, at all costs avoid using passive verbs, never *ever* break up a compound verb with an adverb—are prescriptive. These rules determine what's correct and then try to get everyone to follow them.

Prescriptive grammar has its benefits, up to a point. It helps us make writing and formal speaking more uniform by providing a common set of rules that we have all agreed to use. Then it's up to your grade school English teacher to force you to memorize these rules and put them into practice when you write.

But there's another kind of grammar out there—descriptive grammar. As its name suggests, descriptive grammar describes how things *are*—how a particular language works and how it may be used. Native speakers of a language have adapted those rules instinctively, without learning them as rules, when they were growing up and learning to speak. But by the time you are in your teens, this won't come to you automatically. In order to learn a foreign language, you'll need to learn grammatical rules as rules.

Sure, improving your pronunciation and building up your vocabulary is important. But you can't do anything with these skills unless you also learn the grammar—how all that vocabulary fits together.

There's a lot to learn in Spanish grammar. Just dealing with verbs requires understanding of the purpose of conjugations and being able to choose one correctly, the difference between subjunctive, indicative, and imperative moods; what are reflexive verbs and when they should be used; and so on. And what about the noun/adjective agreement, a vast array of pronouns to choose from, question words that change in meaning at the drop of an accent mark?

But learning grammar doesn't have to be boring. As you go through this book, keep in mind that what you're learning is key to being able to make the Spanish language your own. For each concept you will learn, you'll get the reasoning for why it works the way it works, how it compares to a similar concept in English, and how you can use it in your own speaking and writing.

This book was meant for a wide variety of audiences. It's a great supplementary reference tool for students who need extra help outside of Spanish class. It's also a great idea for those who studied Spanish years ago but are beginning to forget and now would like to brush up on what they learned. Another audience for this book are those who grew up speaking Spanish at home or with friends but never learned Spanish grammar in a classroom setting. This book will give you the grammatical background for a language you know how to speak but maybe aren't as comfortable as you'd like to be when it comes to reading or writing.

Whatever your reasons for picking up *The Everything® Spanish Grammar Book,* I hope you enjoy learning more about Spanish grammar and have the opportunity to put it into practice soon. So sit down, learn the concepts, and then go out there and use what you've learned. In today's world, Spanish is everywhere you turn. Don't be afraid to open your mouth and start speaking. Good luck!

CHAPTER 1
Welcome to the World of Spanish

IN ORDER TO UNDERSTAND the Spanish language and how it works, it is instructive to trace its roots and learn about its origins. Spanish grew and evolved from a spoken dialect that had emerged from a mixture of Latin vernacular and other languages. Over time, the language spread from a small region in Spain known as Castile to cover most of the Iberian Peninsula, and then pushed on to the Americas and Pacific islands like Philippines and Guam. Today, Spanish is the native language of about 350–500 million people, the third most-popular language (following Mandarin Chinese and English).

A Romance Language

Most people are aware that Spanish is a Romance language, but what does this mean? The term has nothing to do with romance and love. *Idiomas romances* are the languages that trace their origins to Latin, the language of Rome.

As you might remember from your ancient history class, in antiquity, Rome had emerged as a powerful city-state that spread throughout Italy and beyond. At its strongest, the Roman Empire controlled a vast territory that encompassed much of Western Europe, North Africa, and Asia Minor—its power reaching from the British Isle in the west to the border of Persia in the east.

As the Roman civilization spread, so did the Latin language spoken by the conquerors. Long after the Roman Empire's collapse, people in what are now France, Spain, Italy, and parts of Switzerland have continued speaking variant forms of Latin. Eventually, these dialects were standardized into modern French, Italian, Spanish, and other Romance languages.

QUESTION?

What are the other Romance languages?
There are quite a few. The more well-known Romance languages are French, Italian, Portuguese, and Romanian. Other languages in this group include Catalan (spoken in northern Spain), Occitan (the language of Provence, France), and Rhaeto-Romanic (a language spoken in southeastern Switzerland).

On the Iberian Peninsula

The history of Spanish follows a similar path. The Roman legions arrived on the Iberian Peninsula (now home to Spain and Portugal) around 200 B.C. The Romans were successful conquerors and colonizers of this region, which they called Hispania. Soon, Hispania became fully incorporated into the Roman Empire. For instance, Seneca (3 B.C.–A.D. 65), who is still revered as a great philosopher and dramatist, was born in Córdoba, Spain. And the region was even home of one of Rome's emperors, Emperor Trajan (A.D. 53–117), who hailed from Italica, a city in southern Spain.

As a result of colonization, Latin spread all over the Iberian Peninsula. By the time the Roman Empire fell in the early fifth century A.D., Latin was well cemented in the region, both as a spoken language and as the language of writing and the Catholic church.

Under Attack

Following the Roman Empire's collapse, the region underwent a period of chaos and decline. Attacks from the north came in waves. First the Vandals and then the Visigoths arrived to pillage and conquer, and the Visigoths managed to stay. They converted to Christianity and assimilated, but their Germanic language affected the local dialects. Certain words and pronunciation patterns not found in Latin were absorbed, while others were dropped. For instance, Spanish spoken in northern and central Spain still retains the sound of "th," which is found in some Germanic languages (including English), but not in other Romance languages or in Latin.

ESSENTIAL

Most Latin nouns have five cases (with five different endings); their usage changes depending on how they are used in the sentence. Luckily for us, Spanish did not retain this usage and the nouns were simplified into one case. The only trace of the cases is found with pronouns.

The Islamic Conquest

Less than 300 years after arrival of the Visigoths, Spain was under attack again, this time from the south. In 711, the first group of Moors from North Africa crossed the Gibraltar strait and clashed with the Spanish. Other attacks followed, and in less than 90 years, the Moors controlled most of what is now Spain.

Al Andalus was a thriving region that boasted the best philosophers, mathematicians, doctors, and poets of its time. Although it was primarily Muslim, Christians and Jews were tolerated as well.

The Language of Castile

Had the Moors conquered all of Spain, Al Andalus might still have been around to this day. However, there was one region that they had failed to capture: Castile. And in Castile, plans were brewing to recapture Spain from the "infidels." Little by little, the Christian armies united and gained strength, and the Moorish armies gave way. It took about 900 years for the Christians to recapture Spain—ten times as long as it had taken the Moors. The last Moorish enclave, Granada, finally fell to the Spanish monarchy in 1492. The language of the monarchy, and of the new nation, was Castilian (*castellano*), the ancestor of modern Spanish.

FACT

In Spanish, *español* means "Spanish," used as an adjective to describe things and people from Spain. You can also use it to refer to the Spanish language, but many people use the term *castellano* when referring to the language they're speaking.

Spanish Literature

During the early Middle Ages, people in different regions of Spain (as well as France and Italy) spoke various dialects like Castilian, but those who were literate wrote in classical Latin. Literacy wasn't common—it was, for the most part, exclusive to the Catholic Church, whose clerics were educated to read the Bible and other religious writings.

Over time, however, the Spanish gradually abandoned this division between speaking and writing, and literature written in Spanish began to appear. One of the earliest known works was the epic poem *Poema del Cid* (*The Poem of El Cid*), which dates back to the twelfth century. It may have been composed orally, but eventually someone wrote it down, and some manuscripts of this work have survived to this day.

Other works of literature followed. During the early fourteenth century, a man by the name of Juan Manuel wrote a collection of morality stories, titled *Conde Lucanor* (*Count Lucanor*). Another pioneering work was *La Celestina* by Fernando Rojas, a story about a go-between (Celestina) and a love affair gone wrong.

The sixteenth century heralded the Golden Age of Spanish literature. Garcilaso de la Vega perfected the Spanish sonnet;

playwrights Lope de Vega and Pedro Calderón de la Barca drew much critical acclaim for their plays. In 1605, Miguel de Cervantes published the first of two parts of *Don Quijote de La Mancha,* a story of an old man from La Mancha who imagines himself to be a great knight and heads out into the world, seeking to do good and fight evil. To this day, many literary critics consider this great work of literature to be the first modern novel, at least in the West and possibly worldwide.

Out to the World

The unification of Spain coincided with another momentous event in Spanish history. In 1492, the explorer Christopher Columbus arrived in the New World and claimed it for the Spanish crown. Columbus explored the island of Hispaniola (now home to Spanish-speaking Dominican Republic and French-Creole Haiti), Cuba, and other Caribbean islands. Spain quickly realized the value of these new possessions and encouraged other explorers to head out to the New World. Soon, Hernando Cortés pushed on and conquered Mexico. Francisco Pizarro defeated the Incas in Peru. Hernando de Soto extended the Spanish presence to Florida. And Álvar Núñez Cabeza de Vaca explored Texas, New Mexico, Arizona, and possibly even California.

In the sixteenth century, Spain controlled Mexico, Central America (excluding Belize), most of South America (except for Brazil, Guyana, French Guiana, and Suriname), much of the Caribbean, the American southwest, the Philippines, and Guam. It also had possessions in North and West Africa.

But soon, the days of glory were over. One by one, Spain began losing its colonies. In the nineteenth century, Simón Bolívar won the independence of Bolivia, Panama, Colombia, Ecuador, Peru, and Venezuela. Mexico gained its independence on September 16, 1821. The final losses came at the end of the Spanish-American War, when Spain lost the Philippines, Guam, and Puerto Rico to the United States, and Cuba won its freedom.

The State of Affairs Today

Although Spain eventually lost its territories, the Spanish language remained in many of these lands. Today, the following twenty-one countries list Spanish as an official language (some of these countries have more than one):

- Argentina
- Bolivia
- Chile
- Colombia
- Costa Rica
- Cuba
- Dominican Republic
- Ecuador
- El Salvador
- Equatorial Guinea
- Guatemala
- Honduras
- Mexico
- Nicaragua
- Panama
- Paraguay
- Peru
- Puerto Rico
- Spain
- Uruguay
- Venezuela

In addition, Spanish still has a presence in the Philippines, Guam, and in the United States. In the U.S. alone, 35 million people are native Spanish speakers. Some of them are recent immigrants, but others are descendants of Spanish and Mexican settlers who arrived long before the Southwest belonged to the United States.

Regional Differences

Because the Spanish language has spread far and wide, there are some regional variations in how it is spoken. A Mexican will have no problem communicating with an Argentinean, but they have different accents, may use some words that are native to their own country or region, and have a slightly different way of saying "you" (Argentinians have a variant form that uses *vos* instead of *tú* as the singular informal form of "you").

CHAPTER 2

Grammar Essentials

IN YOUR STUDIES OF SPANISH GRAMMAR, it might be helpful to start by getting an overview of grammar, and how it works in English as well as in Spanish. Remember, you're not starting from scratch. You already know a lot about grammar because you can speak and write in English.

Just Like English

Despite what it might seem, Spanish and English aren't all that different. Although English isn't a Romance language, it was heavily influenced by one. England hadn't been a part of the Roman Empire for long, so Latin didn't really get a chance to spread to the local populations. However, when in 1066 French-speaking Normans invaded England and took control, their language merged with Old English, a Germanic tongue, to form what we today can recognize as English.

Moreover, during the Middle Ages and up to the twentieth century, education in Britain included the study of Latin, which might explain why English is now full of long vocabulary words like "excoriate," "penultimate," and "prevaricate" (or, more simply, "criticize," "next to the last," and "lie").

Blueprint of a Sentence

To begin, let's first look at the structure of the sentence and how it works, and then look at the parts of speech that may make up the sentence. Each sentence is made up of two main parts: subject and predicate. Think of the subject as the hero of the sentence. It's the word or phrase that does the action or carries the description. The predicate is the rest—the action. Generally, but not always, the subject will come before the predicate.

Subject	Predicate
My friends and I	go to the movies every Friday.
The girl that I had seen last Friday	isn't at home today.
Many students	take Spanish in the morning.
We	like it.

Note that the subject answers the question "who or what?" and the predicate answers what the subject is or does. Take the simplest sentence, "We like it." Who likes it? *We* do—so *we* is the subject. We do what? We *like it*—here, *like it* is the predicate. Who isn't at home today? The girl that I had seen last Friday. The girl that I had seen last Friday is what? She isn't at home today.

The predicate always includes a verb or verb phrase and may also include a complement. In the previous example, the predicate *like it* is made up of the verb *like* and the complement *it*. Some verbs can stand alone, without a complement; others cannot.

Parts of Speech

Subjects and predicates can be further broken down into parts of speech. Spanish and English grammar identifies eight major elements:

noun	*sustantivo*
pronoun	*pronombre*
adjective	*adjetivo*
verb	*verbo*
adverb	*adverbio*
preposition	*preposición*
conjunction	*conjunción*
interjection	*interjección*

Even if you can't tell the difference between these terms, when you speak you intuitively know which are which and how they should be used. The following sections will define these parts of speech so that as you start learning Spanish grammar, these words will not intimidate you.

Name a Noun

Let's start with nouns. A noun may be any of the following:

- **Thing:** computer, desk, pen
- **Person:** mother, John, student
- **Place:** beach, city, Spain, world
- **Concept:** truth, awareness, behavior

If you can match up a word with an article (the, a, or an), it's definitely a noun, but not all nouns can have one: proper names like John and Spain don't take on articles in English.

A Pro with Pronouns

The first thing to remember about pronouns is that they are replacements for nouns or noun phrases. When you keep talking about the same noun, you might get sick of constantly repeating it, so you resort to a pronoun:

John went home. He went home.

Give James a drink. Give him a drink. Give it to him.

Rita's car is red. Her car is red.

I will do it myself.

In these examples, "he," "him," "it," "her," and "myself" are personal pronouns. That is, they work to replace specific nouns. Here's how personal pronouns are categorized in English:

- **Subject pronouns** replace the subject of the sentence. In English, these are "I," "you," "he," "she," "it," "we," and "they."
- **Object pronouns** represent the object noun or phrase. In English, these are "me," "you," "him," "her," "it," "us," and "them."
- **Possessive pronouns** show ownership. In English, these are "my," "mine," "your," "yours," "his," "her," "hers," "its," "our," "ours," "their," and "theirs."
- **Reflexive pronouns** signal that the subject and the object are one and the same. In English, reflexive pronouns are "myself," "yourself," "himself," "herself," "itself," "ourselves," "yourselves," and "themselves."

Other types of pronouns might not be as easily recognizable because they don't necessarily replace a particular noun. Can you figure out which words in the following examples are pronouns?

That was a great movie.

I know who it is you like.

The calculator, which I had used on Friday, is now missing.

What was that noise?

I have everything I need.

I like them both.

They love each other.

The pronouns here are "that," "who," "which," "what," "everything," "both," and "each other." Here is how these pronouns are categorized:

Demonstrative pronouns *demonstrate* or point something out. In English, demonstrative pronouns are: this, that, these, and those. The word "this" in "I like this" is a good example of a demonstrative pronoun. As you can see, it replaces the thing or object which is liked.

Relative pronouns *relate* or connect groups of words to nouns or other pronouns. In English, relative pronouns include: who, whoever, whom, which, that, and whose. For example, in the phrase "I like who you like," the pronoun "who" relates "I" and "you like."

Many of the **interrogative pronouns** are identical to relative pronouns, but they are used differently–to *interrogate,* or ask questions. In English, interrogative pronouns include who, whom, which, whose, and what. In the question "who do you like?" "who" is an interrogative pronoun. Note that in the answer, this pronoun will be replaced by a noun again.

Indefinite pronouns are non-personal pronouns that work as nouns. There are quite a few indefinite pronouns, and many can also be used as adjectives. A few examples in English are: all, none, any, some, everyone, someone, no one, much, little, few, everything, nothing, and something.

Reciprocal pronouns show a mutual relationship between two subjects. In English, there are only two pairs of reciprocal pronouns: "each other" and "one another."

ALERT

Remember that a pronoun must represent—and not describe!—a noun or noun phrase. In the phrase, "this sentence," "this" is not a demonstrative pronoun, because it describes the noun "sentence." In the phrase, "I like this," "this" replaces the *thing* I like, and is therefore a pronoun.

Fun and Easy Adjectives

Pronouns replace nouns, and adjectives describe or modify them. Take a look at the following phrases. Can you tell which ones are adjectives?

I'm always glad to see the pretty flowers.

A healthy child is a happy child.

That house has been empty for many years.

In these examples, "pretty," "healthy," "happy," "that," and "many" are all adjectives. As you can see, in English an adjective generally comes before the noun it describes.

Verb: Action

At their simplest, verbs are words that signal action or being (think of it as inaction). Action verbs describe what someone or something does, whether it's in the past, present, or future:

I *walked* all the way home.

We *talk* often.

She *will finish* her homework later.

Verbs that show a state of being are known as linking verbs: They link or show the relationship between the subject and the object:

Jenny is a student.

That place looks homey.

It feels right.

One sub-group of linking verbs are modal verbs–verbs that express mood (can, may, must ought, shall, should) or verb tense (will and would). Modal verbs behave very irregularly. For example, verbs like "can" only exist in the present tense.

Adverb

It's no coincidence that the word "adverb" has the root "verb"–one of the adverb's main roles is modifying or describing the verb. Here are a few examples of adverbs:

You walk quickly.

I often see you.

Do it carefully.

In these examples, "quickly," "often," and "carefully" are adverbs. Note that many of the adverbs in English are formed by adding the suffix "-ly" to an adjective. In addition to modifying a verb, an adverb may modify an adjective or another adverb:

Do it very carefully.

It's a wonderfully calm night.

In the first sentence, the adverb "very" modifies another adverb, "carefully." In the second, "wonderfully" is an adverb that modifies the adjective "calm," which in turn describes the noun "night."

In Position: Prepositions

Think of prepositions as words that signal position (physical or otherwise) of a noun or pronoun:

I was looking for you.

She is at work.

The box was inside the house.

Here, the prepositions "for," "at," and "inside" explain where the noun is or how it's related to another noun (in the case of the first example). Together with the noun and article, a preposition makes up the prepositional phrases, "for you," "at work," and "inside the house." The entire prepositional phrase functions as a complement of the verb. Without the prepositional phrase, the sentences serving as examples would not have been complete.

Conjunctions and Interjections

Conjunctions and interjections play a secondary role in sentences. Conjunctions are words "at a junction"–words that join or relate words or phrases. In English, conjunctions are divided into three groups:

- **Coordinating conjunctions:** and, but, or, nor, for, so, and yet.
- **Correlative conjunctions:** conjunctions that work in pairs, like either/or and if/then.
- **Subordinating conjunctions:** conjunctions that connect a subordinate clause to the rest of the sentence. There are quite a few of these in English; a few examples are: however, since, because, and whether.

In Agreement

Because grammar governs the role of words in a sentence, it also covers agreement (or correspondence) between words in gender, number, case, and person. In English, agreement is rarely an issue because our language doesn't rely on a whole lot of word endings to communicate information about gender (male, female, or neuter), number (singular or plural), case (role of a noun in a sentence, like whether it's a subject or an object), and person (first, second, or third). For instance, English nouns don't have gender, which means they don't have to agree in gender with articles, adjectives, or any other words. And even in plural form, adjectives and articles do not change:

The red pen.

The red pens.

In Spanish, agreement will require more of your attention. Nouns and pronouns have a particular gender (each one is either feminine or masculine) as well as number, and when paired with articles and adjectives, the endings will change accordingly:

El coche rojo (the red car)

Los coches rojos (the red cars)

La manzana roja (the red apple)

Las manzanas rojas (the red apples)

FACT

In grammar, "person" has to do with how a noun or pronoun is addressed. In first person, the speaker addresses himself: *I am. We are.* In second person, the speaker is addressing another person or people: *You are.* In third person, the speaker is talking about someone or something: *He is. She is. It is. They are.*

In English, the verb does not need to agree in person or number with its subject (one exception is adding "-s" to verbs in third person singular of present tense). In Spanish, the verb must be conjugated according to the person and number of its subject:

Yo camino (I walk)

Tú caminas (you walk)

José camina (José walks)

Nosotros caminamos (we walk)

Tenses and Moods

Spanish verbs are conjugated not only according to person and number, but also according to tense and mood. Whereas English verbs only have four forms–present (take), past (took), present participle (taking), and past participle (taken)–Spanish verbs have quite a lot more, as evidenced by the hefty verb books available for purchase. To keep track of all the different endings, it helps to be sure you understand how tenses and moods work.

Speaking of Time

Languages rely on verb tenses to indicate when the action is taking place, whether the action is ongoing or finite, and whether it's concrete or conditional (something that "would" be done). In English, as well as in Spanish, the tenses include the present, past, future, and conditional, and each category might have more than one tense. For example, the Spanish language has two simple past tenses, preterite and imperfect.

In addition, both English and Spanish employ compound tenses. In English, compound tenses are formed by the verb "to have" and the past participle form of another verb:

I *had gone* there yesterday.

I *have taken* the test already.

I probably *will have lost* it by tomorrow.

In Spanish, the equivalent tenses are formed with the verb *haber* and the past participle.

When a verb isn't conjugated by tense, we use the infinitive form. In English, infinitives are formed with "to": to walk, to talk, to understand. In Spanish, infinitives have one of three endings: –ar, –er, –ir. Knowing the infinitive form will help you conjugate the verb correctly.

No Need for Mood Rings

In addition to tenses, verbs are also conjugated according to mood. English and Spanish both have three moods:

Indicative mood: Used to express objective statements. This is the most commonly used mood, particularly in English.

Subjunctive mood: Used to express statements that are in doubt or hypothetical. In the following sentence, the verb "were" is in the subjunctive mood: "If I were younger, I would be able to run quickly." The subjunctive mood is rarely used in English, but is common in Spanish.

Imperative mood: The mood of command. Examples are: Take this one! Give me the rest! Don't put it there! Notice that in giving commands, you drop the subject "you." The same is true in Spanish, but the verb is conjugated differently.

Practice Makes Perfect

Break down the following sentences into subject and predicate:

1. The cars I saw parked outside were not very clean.
2. I wanted to buy a jacket that would fit me well.
3. Students and their parents eagerly waited their turn.

4. It rained frequently.
5. Everybody in the audience clapped.

What part of speech is each of the following words?

1. interesting __________
2. huh __________
3. made __________
4. humor __________
5. to blame __________

To check your answers, refer to the answer key in Appendix D.

CHAPTER 3

Start with the Basics

NOW THAT YOU'VE GOT THE GRAMMAR essentials down, let's begin learning Spanish! This chapter is a review of the basics: the alphabet, standard pronunciation, using the accent mark, and numbers. Even if you're already familiar with these topics, it won't hurt to review them so that you are ready to move on to other concepts.

Learn Your ABCs

If you remember the English alphabet, learning the Spanish version will be a snap: Because the Spanish alphabet is almost identical, all you have to do is memorize the pronunciation of each letter.

FACT

Prior to 1994, the Spanish alphabet was three letters longer, because it included three letter combinations: CH ("cheh"), LL ("EH-yeh" or "EH-zheh"), and RR ("EH-rr-eh). In older Spanish dictionaries listings beginning with CH, LL, and RR have their own separate sections.

The Spanish Alphabet	
letter	pronunciation
A	ah
B	beh
C	seh
D	deh
E	eh
F	EF-eh
G	heh
H	AH-cheh
I	ee
J	HOH-tah
K	kah
L	EH-leh
M	EH-meh
N	EH-neh
Ñ	EH-nyeh
O	oh
P	pei
Q	koo
R	EH-reh
S	EH-seh
T	teh
U	oo
V	veh, beh
W	DOH-bleh veh, DOH-bleh beh
X	EH-kis
Y	ee GRIEH-gah
Z	ZEH-tah, SEH-tah

Pronunciation Guide

The basics of Spanish pronunciation aren't difficult to master—only a few sounds don't have an equivalent in English. And learning to read is much easier too because Spanish is written as it's spoken. For example, in Spanish the vowel letter A is always read as "ah." In contrast, the English vowel letter A can represent several vowel sounds: "ei," "e," "ah," and so on.

Pronunciation of Spanish Letters

letter	pronunciation	examples
A	"a" in "father"	*mano* (hand)
B	"b" in "box"	*bella* (pretty)
C	"c" in "call"	*caja* (box)
	"c" in "city" (followed by "e" or "i")	*cine* (movies)
D	"d" in "deck"	*día* (day)
E	"e" in "pen"	*pera* (pear)
F	"f" in "fine"	*fe* (faith)
G	"g" in "go"	*ganar* (to win, earn)
	a hard "h" (followed by "e" or "i")	*gemelo* (twin)
H	mute, except in "ch"	*hola* (hello)
I	"i" in "seen"	*listo* (ready)
J	a hard "h"	*justo* (just, fair)
K	"k" in "karma" (in words of foreign origin)	*koala* (koala)
L	"l" in "lick"	*lado* (side)
M	"m" in "more"	*mayo* (May)
N	"n" in "nickel"	*nada* (nothing)

Pronunciation of Spanish Letters (continued)		
Ñ	similar to "ni" in "onion"	*niño* (baby, boy)
O	"o" in "more"	*mosca* (fly)
P	"p" in "open"	*país* (country)
Q	"k" in "king"	*queso* (cheese)
R	"tt" in "matter"	*oro* (gold)
S	"s" in "smart"	*sonar* (to ring)
T	"t" in "stay"	*tamaño* (size)
U	"oo" in "boot"	*tuyo* (yours)
V	"b" in "box"	vencer (to overcome)
W	"w" in "way" (in words of foreign origin)	*waterpolo* (waterpolo)
X	"x" in "taxes"	*exilio* (exile)
Y	like "y" in "yellow"	*yo* (I)
Z	like "s" in "smart"	*zapato* (shoe)

ALERT

The pronunciation guide provided here is applicable to standard Spanish spoken in South America. Some regional variations are mentioned here as well, but they're meant as examples and aren't intended to be thorough.

A Few Helpful Hints

Here are a few additional points to review:

B and **V:** In many parts of the Spanish-speaking world, B and V are pronounced the same. At the beginning of the word or following M or N, they're pronounced like the "b" in "box." In all other cases, the Spanish B and V are actually modified to a soft "b" sound, with lips barely meeting. There's no equivalent of this sound in English, and you'll have to practice listening to it in Spanish and try to reproduce it.

D: Pronunciation of D also depends on its place in the word. At the beginning or after L or N, it's pronounced like the "d" in "deck." In all other cases, it sounds more like the "th" in "mother."

X: In words of American Indian origin, X may be pronounced as a hard "h" or "sh."

Y: People in the Río de la Plata region (Argentina and Uruguay) pronounce Y (as well as the LL combination) like the "s" in "treasure."

Z: Pronunciation of Z varies from country to country. In some parts of Spain, it's pronounced like "th" in "think." In a few areas, it's pronounced like the "z" in "zoo." In most of Latin America and Andalusia (Southern Spain), it's pronounced exactly the same as S.

Letter Combinations

To complete the guide to pronunciation, let's review the letter combinations used to represent additional sounds:

CH: Just as in English, these two letters combine to form the sound of "ch" in "chin."

GU and **QU:** Just as in English, "q" always comes in combination with "u," but the result is slightly different–the U remains silent. For example, *que* (that) is pronounced keh; *quince* (fifteen) is pronounced KEEN-seh. GU works the same way: *guerra* (war) is pronounced GEH-rrah. In GU words where the U is pronounced, it's written with two dots (an umlaut) to indicate the change in pronunciation. For example, *vergüenza* (shame), pronounced behr-goo-EHN-sah.

LL: Generally, this combination serves to represent the sound "y" in "yellow." In Argentina and Uruguay, it is pronounced like the "s" in "measure."

RR: This combination represents a long rolling "r" sound that does not have an equivalent in English. A single R at the beginning of a word also represents this sound.

UA: In this vowel combination, the letter U becomes shorter, forming a sound similar to "w" in "war." For example, *puerta* (door) is pronounced PWER-tah.

Showing Stress

Because Spanish is written just like it sounds, spelling is rarely a problem. The only issue that may pose some difficulty is the use of the accent mark (´).

Accent marks aren't arbitrary. They're used to show which syllable should be stressed in words that don't follow the standard stress pattern. This pattern is easy to learn and can be described by two simple rules:

1. If a word ends in a vowel, N, or S, it is generally stressed on the second to last syllable. For example: *carta* (CAHR-tah), letter; *manchas* (MAHN-chahs), stains; *cantan* (CAHN-tahn), they sing.

2. If a word ends in a consonant other than N or S, it is generally stressed on the last syllable. For example: *merced* (mehr-CEHD), mercy; *cantar* (cahn-TAHR), to sing; *metal* (meh-TAHL), metal.

If the stress does not obey these rules, it must be signaled by adding an accent mark over the vowel in the correctly stressed syllable. For example, the word *útil,* useful, should be stressed on the last syllable, because it ends with an L. However, because the correct pronunciation of this word is OO-teel (and not oo-TEEL), an accent is placed over the vowel U. Here are a few other examples of words that require an accent mark because they do not follow the standard stress pattern:

fácil	easy
información	information
típico	typical
millón	million

Accent marks may also be used to distinguish words that are spelled and pronounced the same but have different meanings. For example, words like "who," "what," and "where" are spelled with an accent mark when they serve as questions, but they lose the accent mark when they are used in the answer. For example:

¿Dónde está el almacén?

Where is the grocery store?

Está donde vive Carlos, en la calle Union.

It's where Carlos lives, on Union Street.

Here are a few common pairs of words that may be distinguished by the presence of the accent mark:

qué (what?)	*que* (what, that)
quién (who?)	*quien* (who, that)
dónde (where?)	*donde* (where, there)
cuándo (when?)	*cuando* (when, then)
cuánto (how much/many?)	*cuanto* (as much/many)
cómo (how?)	*como* (as, like)
sí (yes)	*si* (if)
sólo (only)	*solo* (alone)
más (more)	*mas* (but)
mí (me)	*mi* (my)

tú (you)	*tu* (your)
él (he)	*el* (the)

Counting Off

Another basic skill is counting. Just as in English, Spanish numbers are organized by tens. To start counting, here is the first set, starting with zero:

0	*cero*	6	*seis*
1	*uno*	7	*siete*
2	*dos*	8	*ocho*
3	*tres*	9	*nueve*
4	*cuatro*	10	*diez*
5	*cinco*		

The next set of numbers includes the teens:		The numbers 20–29 are also written as one word:	
11	*once*	20	*veinte*
12	*doce*	21	*veintiuno*
13	*trece*	22	*veintidós*
14	*catorce*	23	*veintitrés*
15	*quince*	24	*veinticuatro*
16	*dieciséis*	25	*veinticinco*
17	*diecisiete*	26	*veintiséis*
18	*dieciocho*	27	*veintisiete*
19	*diecinueve*	28	*veintiocho*
		29	*veintinueve*

Even when you use a number as an adjective describing how many of something there is, the number's ending does not change according to the gender of the noun. For example: *cuatro hijos; cuatro hijas*. However, *uno* and other numbers ending in *uno* do change in gender. For example: *un padre, una madre; veintiún padres; veintiuna madre*. The same is true for hundreds: *doscientos edificios, doscientas casas.*

Following 30, numbers are simply written as phrases: "thirty and one," "thirty and two," and so on. All you need to memorize are the numbers divisible by 10:

30	*treinta*	70	*setenta*
40	*cuarenta*	80	*ochenta*
50	*cincuenta*	90	*noventa*
60	*sesenta*		

Here are a few examples of numbers between 30 and 99:

32	*treinta y dos*	87	*ochenta y siete*
45	*cuarenta y cinco*	99	*noventa y nueve*
51	*cincuenta y uno*		

If you want to keep counting, the next number is *cien,* 100. Then, numbers continue up to 199 with *ciento* plus the rest of the number. Here are a few examples:

125	*ciento veinticinco*	189	*ciento ochenta y nueve*
146	*ciento cuarenta y seis*		

QUESTION?

When should I use *cien* and when *ciento?*
Use *cien* when the number is exactly a hundred—either to say "hundred" or a hundred of something. For example: *cien mil,* a hundred thousand. If the number is a hundred and something, use *ciento.*

The numbers from 200 to 999 work the same: You start with the hundreds, then add the rest of the number. For example, 348 is *trescientos cuarenta y ocho.*

200	*doscientos*	600	*seiscientos*
300	*trescientos*	700	*setecientos*
400	*cuatrocientos*	800	*ochocientos*
500	*quinientos*	900	*novecientos*

And don't forget that when these numbers are used to count nouns, the ending can change to feminine according to rules of agreement. For example: *cuatrocientas casas* (four hundred houses).

The pattern of forming the number by going from hundreds to tens to ones continues the higher you go. For example, 1998 is *mil novecientos noventa y ocho.* Here's the rest of the vocabulary you might need to keep counting up:

1,000	*mil*	1,000,000	*millón*
2,000	*dos mil*	2,000,000	*dos millones*

For the Nth Time

Numbers used for counting (one, two, three) or as adjectives (one book, two books, three books) are known as ordinal numbers. But there's another group of numbers: cardinal numbers. Cardinal numbers don't deal with quantity—they serve to indicate the order of something: first, second, third, and so on. In English, all cardinal numbers following the first three end with –th, so they are easily recognized. In Spanish, the pattern is only slightly more complicated. You'll have to memorize the first ten:

first	*primero*
second	*segundo*
third	*tercero*
fourth	*cuarto*
fifth	*quinto*
sixth	*sexto*
seventh	*séptimo*
eighth	*octavo*
ninth	*noveno*
tenth	*décimo*

Starting with "eleventh," Spanish switches back to cardinal numbers, so "the eleventh hour" would be translated as *la hora once.*

Practice Makes Perfect

Some of the following words need an accent mark. Add an accent mark where necessary.

1. *cantabamos*
2. *dificil*
3. *camarones*
4. *recomendacion*
5. *pontelo*
6. *voluntad*

Write out the following numbers:

1. 5 ______________
2. 16 ______________
3. 27 ______________
4. 202 ______________
5. 344 ______________
6. 1998 ______________

Add the correct ordinal number, spelled out. For example, (3) *coche* would be *el tercer coche.*

1. (4) *libro* ______________
2. (10) *historia* ______________
3. (1) *comunidad* ______________
4. (8) *horario* ______________
5. (9) *número* ______________
6. (7) *página* ______________

To check your answers, refer to the answer key in Appendix D.

CHAPTER 4

About Nouns

A NOUN, OR SUSTANTIVO, is a word that refers to a person, animal, thing, or idea. Nouns can be accompanied by articles (a, an, the) and described by adjectives. A noun may be the subject of the sentence, in which case it takes on the action of the verb, or it can serve as an object or as part of a prepositional phrase.

Divided by Gender

Only a few English nouns have a particular gender: for example, you know that "sister" is feminine and "brother" is masculine. But what about a noun like "cookie"? It doesn't have a gender.

In Spanish, noun genders work a little differently. *Hermana* is feminine and *hermano* is masculine, so nouns representing people work similarly. However, the difference is that even nouns like "cookie" have a gender (in this case, *galleta* is a feminine noun). All nouns in Spanish can be divided into two groups: feminine and masculine.

This doesn't mean that people who speak Spanish see cookies as having particularly feminine qualities. The gender of any particular noun has nothing to do with the object itself–it's a grammatical construction that allows nouns to agree with other parts of speech. So if you see a noun in context, you can figure out whether it's masculine or feminine by checking the ending of its article or adjective. If these clues aren't available, you can probably make a guess based on a few rules of thumb presented here.

Check the Ending

The clue to whether a noun is masculine or feminine can be found in its ending. The first rule of thumb is that some masculine nouns end in an –o, and many feminine nouns end in an –a.

Masculine	Feminine
el caso (case)	*la casa* (house)
el gasto (expense)	*la plata* (silver)
el techo (roof)	*la mosca* (fly)
el niño (boy)	*la niña* (girl)

One important exception to this rule: Nouns that end with –ma, like *el problema* (problem), are masculine.

ALERT

The easiest way to keep track of which nouns are masculine and which are feminine is to memorize them along with their definite article (the). As you'll learn in the next section, masculine nouns agree with the masculine article *el* and feminine nouns with the feminine article *la*.

If the rule of thumb doesn't apply, check to see if the noun has one the following endings. If it does, the noun is most likely feminine.

–dad	*la verdad* (truth)
–ión	*la contemplación* (contemplation)
–tad	*la libertad* (liberty)
–tud	*la quietud* (quiet)
–ie	*la especie* (species)
–sis	*la tesis* (thesis)

–ez	*la vejez* (old age)
–triz	*la cicatriz* (scar)
–umbre	*la certidumbre* (certainty)

With all other endings, you can probably assume that the noun is masculine. Unless, of course, it's one of the exceptions to the rule.

Learn the Exceptions

Every rule has its exceptions, and there are a few nouns that don't follow the general rules of grammatical gender:

Masculine	Feminine
el día (day)	*la clase* (class)
el planeta (planet)	*la gente* (people)
el mapa (map)	*la cama* (bed)
el sofá (sofa)	*la pluma* (pen)
el avión (plane)	

Representing Gender

And what about nouns referring to people, which do have gender? In Spanish, nouns that represent people do match the gender of the person referred to. In some cases, the two words are completely different:

el hombre (man)	*la mujer* (woman)

Other nouns simply change the ending:

el tío (uncle)	*la tía* (aunt)
el primo (cousin)	*la prima* (cousin)

el abogado (lawyer)	*la abogada* (lawyer)
el niño (boy)	*la niña* (girl)
And in some cases, both genders retain the same ending:	
el dentista (dentist)	*la dentista* (dentist)
el pianista (pianist)	*la pianista* (pianist)
el estudiante (student)	*la estudiante* (student)

ESSENTIAL

Here's another exception to remember: there are a few feminine nouns that take on the article *el* in the singular. The reason for this is simple: Feminine nouns that begin with a stressed "ah" syllable can't take on the article *la*—the two "ah"s will get swallowed up into one sound—so to make the article clear, you switch to *el.* For example: *el águila* (the eagle), *las águilas* (the eagles).

Forming Plurals

Conveniently enough, in Spanish a noun is made plural by adding an –s or –es, just as you do in English. If a noun ends in a vowel, use the –s ending:

carta (letter)	*cartas* (letters)
abuelo (grandfather)	*abuelos* (grandfathers)
guante (glove)	*guantes* (gloves)
Nouns ending in a consonant take on –es to form a plural:	
comedor (dining room)	*comedores* (dining rooms)
habilidad (ability)	*habilidades* (abilities)
matón (killer)	*matones* (killers)

Dropping the Accent Mark

As you can see from the example of *matón/matones*, making a noun plural may affect the use of the accent mark. Remember, words ending with a vowel, S, or N generally have a stressed second-to-last syllable, and exceptions must employ the accent mark to show where the stress falls. Because *matón* is pronounced "mah-TOHN," and not "MAH-tohn," the accent mark is employed to indicate correct pronunciation. However, by adding –es the syllable "ton" becomes second-to-last, thus making the accent mark unnecessary in the plural.

Spelling Modifications

It's also important to remember that adding the plural ending may affect the spelling of the word. For instance, a final Z will change to C, in order to avoid combination ZE, which does not occur in Spanish: *el pez* (fish), *los peces* (fishes).

QUESTION?

If a plural noun refers to a group of both genders, which ending should be used?

Plural nouns that refer to a mixed group of both genders retain a masculine ending. For example, even if you've got one male cousin and twelve female cousins, you will refer to them collectively as *los primos*.

Other Exceptions

As you know, some English nouns don't have a singular and a plural form. For example, the word "elk" can be either singular or plural. The only way to know is through context. A few Spanish words behave the same way. For example, a compound word where the second part of the word is plural will retain the same ending, whether the noun is singular or plural: *paraguas* (umbrella, literally "for water") is *el paraguas* in the singular and *los paraguas* in the plural.

Other nouns only exist in the singular form, even though they refer to more than one person or object. The best example is "people" or *gente*. Although the noun refers to multiple individuals, the form both in English and in Spanish remains singular.

Definite Articles

English only has one definite article: "the." The article is used with nouns to make them specific (or definite): the book, the job, the idea. In a sense, Spanish also has one definite article, but the article has four forms because it must agree in gender and number with the noun that it precedes:

el	masculine/singular	*el libro* (the book)
la	feminine/singular	*la mancha* (the stain)
los	masculine/plural	*los libros* (the books)
las	feminine/plural	*las manchas* (the stains)

Note that the masculine/singular form el may appear as a contraction:

a + el	*al* (to the)
de + el	*del* (from the)

The contraction is formed because the vowel at the end of the preposition merges with the vowel at the beginning of the word *el*. This does not occur with the other forms of the article:

a la playa (to the beach)	*al cine* (to the movies)
de la playa (from the beach)	*del cine* (from the movies)

Indefinite Articles

An indefinite article preceding a noun indicates nonspecific (indefinite) objects: A book is an unspecified book; an idea is an unspecified idea. In English, the definite article "a" ("an" before a vowel) is only used with singular nouns. If there's more than just a book, we say "books" or give the number of books: two books, some books, a few books.

In Spanish, the indefinite article can be used with singular as well as with plural objects. Because it must agree in gender and number with the noun it precedes, the indefinite article also has four forms:

un	masculine/singular	*un libro* (a book)
una	feminine/singular	*una mancha* (a stain)
unos	masculine/plural	*unos libros* (some books)
unas	feminine/plural	*unas manchas* (some stains)

FACT

The indefinite article means nothing more than "one." A book is really one book; an idea is just one idea. In Spanish, this is more obvious because *un* and *una* can be translated as "one."

Choosing the Right Article

For the most part, articles in English and Spanish correspond to each other: "the" usually translates as *el, la, los,* or *las,* and "a" or "an" translate as *un* or *una*. However, there are some instances where article usage in Spanish differs.

Dropping the Indefinite Article

The indefinite article is not used as frequently as it is in English. One general rule is that when substituting "a" for "one" sounds strange, you drop it in Spanish. For example, you don't need it when describing someone's profession:

Ella es enfermera.

She is a nurse.

Quiero ser millonario.

I want to be a millionaire.

The indefinite article is also dropped in exclamations beginning with *qué:*

¡Qué alegría!

What a joy!

¡Qué chiste más gracioso!

What an amusing joke!

The indefinite article is also dropped after *con* (with) and *sin* (without):

Escribo con pluma.

I write with a pen.

Sin duda, es la mejor idea.

Without a doubt, it's the best idea.

Body Parts

In English, you would use the possessive pronoun "my" to refer to a part of your body. In Spanish, however, parts of the body are preceded by definite articles, whether you're talking about your own body or about someone else's:

Me rompí la pierna.

I broke my leg.

A ella le gusta cepillarse el cabello.

She likes to brush her hair.

As you'll see in the following sections, expressions of possession also affect article use.

QUESTION?

What are proper nouns?
Proper nouns are "name" nouns. Jill, Smith, London, and Shorty are all examples of proper nouns. To help you make a distinction, think of it this way: "city" is a noun, but "London" is the name of a city, so it's a proper noun.

The Rules of Possession

"Possession" is a big word for a simple concept: a relationship of ownership. If you ask the question "whose?" the answer–mine, Jane's, the high school students'–is the possessor.

In English, possession is indicated by adding an apostrophe and "s" ('s) to the noun representing the possessor:

Jane's car (car owned by Jane)

Student's notebooks (notebooks of the student)

As you can see, in the English construction, the possessor (Jane, student) comes before what is possessed (car, notebooks). In Spanish, this construction does not exist. Instead, people use the Spanish equivalent of the preposition "of" (*de*), and say *el coche de Jane* (literally, "the car of Jane"). In this construction, the object possessed always comes before the possessor:

los zapatos de Enrique

Enrique's shoes

el libro de la chica con pelo negro

the girl with black hair's book

la amiga de la hermana de Diana

Diana's sister's friend

In Spanish, the object or person possessed (shoes, girl, friend) carry a definite article. Possession can also be signaled with possessive pronouns, covered in the next chapter.

Practice Makes Perfect

Indicate whether each of the following nouns is masculine or feminine:

1. *árbol* __________
2. *dieta* __________
3. *navidad* __________
4. *malecón* __________
5. *solución* __________
6. *tienda* __________
7. *problema* __________
8. *paraguas* __________
9. *ajedrez* __________
10. *especie* __________

Write down the plural form:

1. *la consecuencia* ________________
2. *el microondas* ________________
3. *un pez* ________________
4. *una cocina* ________________
5. *el ratón* ________________
6. *un matador* ________________
7. *la merced* ________________
8. *un café* ________________

Insert the correct definite and indefinite article, where necessary (and don't forget about the rules of agreement):

1. *Me gusta tomar una siesta* ________________ *domingos.*
2. *Escribí* ________________ *poemas para ella.*
3. *Me duele* ________________ *cabeza.*
4. *Mi papá es* ________________ *abogado.*
5. *Tengo* ________________ *regalo para ti.*
6. *Ya pasaron* ________________ *semanas desde que te vi por* ________________ *última vez.*
7. ________________ *Sánchez me invitaron a su casa a cenar con* ________________ *ellos.*
8. *¡Qué* ________________ *bebé más dulce!*

Translate into Spanish:

1. Maria's house ________________
2. Ricardo's brother's wife ________________
3. the class teacher ________________

4. the doctor's patients ____________
5. the children's toys ____________
6. today's lesson ____________

To check your answers, refer to the answer key in Appendix D.

CHAPTER 5

Making Sense of Pronouns

A PRONOUN IS A GRAMMATICAL DESIGNATION for words used to replace nouns and noun phrases. Some pronouns are easy to recognize: ella (she) is a pronoun that may be used instead of Marina or la chica de la calle Central (the girl from Central Street). Other pronouns are more difficult because they're really other parts of speech working as pronouns. For example, compare Mucha gente cree que el castellano es difícil de aprender (Many people believe Spanish is difficult to learn) with Muchos lo creen (Many believe that). In the second example, *muchos* is an adjective that serves as a pronoun referring to *gente* and *lo* is a pronoun referring to *que el castellano es difícil de aprender*. Confused? Don't despair. This chapter will help you see how pronouns work.

From Noun to Pronoun

In the simplest terms, a pronoun takes the place of a noun to make a switch from a specific noun or noun phrase to a more "generic" word. Pronouns don't carry meaning in and of themselves. What they do is refer to something that has already been said. For example, "the gray cat" can be referred to simply as "it," as long as it is clear what the pronoun "it" refers to.

There are eight types of pronouns in Spanish:

1. **Personal pronouns** (*pronombres personales*): Pronouns that replace personal nouns, like *yo* (I) and *nosotros* (us).

2. **Possessive pronouns** (*pronombres posesivos*): Pronouns that represent the possessor in a possessive construction, like *mi* (my) and *tuyo* (yours).

3. **Demonstrative pronouns** (*pronombres demonstrativos*): Pronouns that demonstrate or refer to a noun, particularly in terms of its location in respect to the speakers, like *éste* (this) and *aquéllas* (those).

4. **Numeral pronouns** (*pronombres numerales*): Numbers used as pronouns, like *primero* (first one) and *par* (pair).

5. **Indefinite pronouns** (*pronombres indefinidos*): Pronouns that refer to nouns in terms of their quantity, like *algún* (some) and *todo* (all).

6. **Relative pronouns** (*pronombres relativos*): *Que* (that), *cual/cuales* (which), and *quien/quienes* (who, that), used as pronouns.

7. **Interrogative pronouns** (*pronombres interrogativos*): Relative pronouns used as question words. To differentiate relative and interrogative pronouns, the latter are spelled with accent marks: *qué, cuál, cuáles, quién,* and *quiénes.*

8. **Exclamation pronouns** (*pronombres exclamativos*): The same five pronouns, but used in exclamations. For example: *¡Qúe bonito!* (How pretty!)

Numeral pronouns, or numerals used as pronouns, are covered in Chapter 3. Relative and interrogative pronouns are reviewed in Chapter 2, which explains the structure of the Spanish question and exclamation.

It's Personal

There are four types of personal pronouns: subject pronouns, direct object pronouns, indirect object pronouns, and reflexive pronouns. Subject pronouns are pronouns representing nouns that serve as the subject of the verb.

Subject Pronouns	
singular	**plural**
yo (I)	*nosotros, nosotras* (we)
tú (you, informal)	*vosotros, vosotras* (you, informal in Spain)
usted (you, formal)	*ustedes* (you)
él, ella, ello (he, she, it)	*ellos, ellas* (they)

Subject pronouns in English and Spanish differ in a few important ways. First of all, subject pronouns are often dropped in Spanish. The explanation is simple: If the verb is present, its ending will reflect the person and number of its subject, so that it is obvious what the subject pronoun would be. This means *yo busco* (I look for) can simply be stated as *busco*. The –o ending makes it clear the subject pronoun is *yo*. Even in the third person singular, where the subject pronoun could be *él, ella, ello,* or *usted,* the pronoun is dropped when the subject is obvious from context:

Dolores es de Madrid. Es madrileña.
Dolores is from Madrid. She is a *madrileña*.

Also note that some of the Spanish subject pronouns reflect the gender of the noun they represent, which does not occur in English (except in the case of "he" and "she"): *nosotras* is a feminine form of "we," *vosotras* is a feminine form of the informal "you" used in Spain, and *ellas* is a feminine form of "they." As you've already learned, when speaking of a mixed-gender group, the masculine form should be used.

ESSENTIAL

The equivalent of "it," *ello,* is a neuter form rarely encountered in modern Spanish. Here's an example of how it might be used: *Como consecuencia de ello, estamos vencidos.* (As a consequence [of it], we're conquered.)

Hey, You!

Arguably the most important difference between subject pronouns (and other personal pronouns) in English and Spanish is the use of the second person pronouns. In English, "you" is used any time you address another person or group of people, regardless of whether you're being casual or polite. In Spanish, you'll need to choose one of several different pronouns depending on the situation at hand.

When addressing one person, you have to choose between a casual and a polite "you." When speaking to friends or people much younger than yourself, you can use the casual form, *tú*. In all other cases, it's best to err on the side of politeness and choose the polite form, *usted*. If the person you're speaking with finds this form too formal, he'll invite you to switch to *tú*. (The verb for speaking in the *tú* form is *tutearse.)*

In most of Argentina and Uruguay, as well as in a few other regions of Latin America, *vos* is used instead of *tú* in addressing a person informally. When this occurs, the verb ending is different as well. For example, in the present tense, "you have" is *vos tenés* and not *tú tienes.*

In the plural, your pronoun usage will depend on whether you're speaking Spanish in Spain or in Latin America. In Spain, there are two more words meaning "you": *vosotros* (or *vosotras* for feminine nouns) is the informal form, the plural equivalent of *tú,* whereas *ustedes* is the more formal version, the plural of *usted.* In Latin America, no distinction is made between formal and informal address in the plural. When speaking to more than one person, Latin Americans always use *ustedes.*

FACT

Usted and *ustedes* were latecomers to Spanish. The word *usted* is an abbreviated version of the phrase *vuestra merced,* "your mercy," which was used to address royalty. Later, the phrase was shortened and its use became more widespread as a polite way of address.

Object Pronouns

Object pronouns are pronouns that receive the action of the verb (for more on how this works, see Chapter 10). In Spanish, object pronouns are divided into two groups: direct object pronouns and indirect object pronouns.

Direct object pronouns replace the direct object. For example:

Yo compré un vestido rojo. Yo lo compré.

I bought a red dress. I bought it.

The direct object answers to the question of "subject + verb + who/what?"

I bought what?

I bought a red dress.

I bought it.

"It" is therefore a direct object pronoun. In Spanish, each subject pronoun has a direct object pronoun equivalent.

Direct Object Pronouns	
singular	**plural**
me (me)	*nos* (us)
te (you, informal)	*os* (you, informal in Spain)
lo, la (you, formal)	*los, las* (you)
lo, la (him, her, it)	*los, las* (them)

The verb may also have an indirect object:

Yo te compré un vestido rojo. Yo te lo compré.

I bought you a red dress. I bought it for you.

The indirect object here, *te,* answers the question, "to whom?" or "for whom?" the action of the verb is performed. Whereas in English, indirect objects may only appear if a direct object is present, in Spanish it's possible to have an indirect object without a direct one there as well.

ALERT

In Spanish, when the objects are in the form of pronouns, they are placed before the verb. When both a direct and an indirect object pronoun are present, the indirect object pronouns comes first, followed by the direct object pronoun and the verb.

The following pronouns serve as indirect objects. Note that in the first and second person, the indirect object pronouns are identical to direct object pronouns.

Indirect Object Pronouns	
singular	**plural**
me (me)	*nos* (us)
te (you, informal)	*os* (you, informal in Spain)
le (you, formal)	*les* (you)
le (him, her, it)	*les* (them)

When the direct and the indirect objects are both pronouns, the indirect object pronouns *le* and *les* change to *se* before *lo, la, los,* and *las*. This is done in order to avoid confusion of saying two similar-sounding words one after another:

Yo se lo compré.

I bought it for her.

Reflexive Pronouns

Reflexive pronouns are used with reflexive verbs to show that the action of the verb is done to the subject of the verb. Take a look at the following example:

Yo me lavo en la ducha.

I wash (myself) in the shower.

Note that the subject pronoun, *yo,* refers to the same person as the reflexive pronoun, *me*. One way to think of this relationship is to remember that the reflexive pronoun reflects back to the subject of the sentence. In English, this is done with pronouns that end with –self and –selves.

Reflexive Pronouns	
singular	**plural**
me (myself)	*nos* (ourselves)
te (yourself, informal)	*os* (yourselves, informal)
se (yourself, formal)	*se* (yourselves)
se (himself, herself, itself)	se (themselves)

In addition to working reflexively, reflexive pronouns may be used reciprocally. In English, this is done by using the phrases "each other" and one another":

Nos queremos mucho.

We love each other a lot.

ESSENTIAL

Many of the verbs that are reflexive in Spanish don't work the same way in English. For example, *me levanto* is translated as "I get up," not "I get up myself." For a review of reflexive verbs, see Chapter 10.

Whose Is It, Anyway?

Possessive pronouns are pronouns that represent the possessor or owner:

Es el sombrero de Jorge. Es su sombrero.

It's Jorge's hat. It's his hat.

Possessive pronouns may work as adjectives modifying a noun, as in the previous example, where *su* describes *sombrero*.

Possessive Pronouns as Adjectives	
singular	**plural**
mi (my)	*nuestro, nuestra, nuestros, nuestras* (our)
tu (your, informal)	*vuestro, vuestra, vuestros, vuestras* (your, informal in Spain)
su (your, formal)	*su* (your)
su (his, her, its)	*su* (their)
Note that the *nuestro* and *vuestro* must agree in number and gender with the object of possession:	
nuestro perro	our dog
nuestra oficina	our office
nuestros perros	our dogs
nuestras oficinas	our offices

On the other hand, *su perro* can mean "your dog" (formal singular or plural), "his dog," "her dog," or "their dog."

Possessive Pronouns as Nouns

In a modified form, possessive pronouns can replace nouns or noun phrases. Take a look at the following example:

Es el sombrero de Jorge. Es su sombrero. Es suyo.

It's Jorge's hat. It's his hat. It's his.

In English, the same word, "his," is used as a possessive adjective and possessive noun (this is not true of all forms, like "my/mine"). In Spanish, the following pronouns are used to replace a possessive noun phrase:

Possessive Pronouns as Nouns				
masculine singular	**feminine singular**	**masculine plural**	**feminine plural**	**English**
el mío	*la mía*	*los míos*	*las mías*	mine
el tuyo (informal)	*la tuya*	*los tuyos*	*las tuyas*	yours
el suyo (formal)	*la suya*	*los suyos*	*las suyas*	yours
el suyo	*la suya*	*los suyos*	*las suyas*	his, hers, its
el nuestro	*la nuestra*	*los nuestros*	*las nuestras*	ours
el vuestro (informal, in Spain)	*la vuestra*	*los vuestros*	*las vuestras*	yours
el suyo (plural)	*la suya*	*los suyos*	*las suyas*	yours
el suyo	*la suya*	*los suyos*	*las suyas*	theirs

To choose the right possessive pronoun, you'll need to consider the possessor as well as the object possessed. The right pronoun will take the form of the possessor, but agree in number and gender with the object possessed:

el colchón de mí	*mi colchón*	*el mío*	my mattress
la computadora de mí	*mi computadora*	*la mía*	my computer
los anteojos de mí	*mis anteojos*	*los míos*	my glasses
las revistas de mí	*mis revistas*	*las mías*	my magazines

el vaso de ti	*tu vaso*	*el tuyo*	your glass
la muñeca de ti	*tu muñeca*	*la tuya*	your doll
los libros de ti	*tus libros*	*los tuyos*	your books
las manzanas de ti	*tus manzanas*	*las tuyas*	your apples

el buzón de usted	*su buzón*	*el suyo*	your mailbox
la multa de usted	*su multa*	*la suya*	your fine
los pañuelos de usted	*sus pañuelos*	*los suyos*	your handkerchiefs
las casas de usted	*sus casas*	*las suyas*	your houses

el lápiz de él	*su lápiz*	*el suyo*	his pencil
la torta de él	*su torta*	*la suya*	his cake
los dulces de él	*sus dulces*	*los suyos*	his candy
las monedas de él	*sus monedas*	*las suyas*	his coins
el chicle de ella	*su chicle*	*el suyo*	her gum
la plata de ella	*su plata*	*la suyo*	her money
las bananas de ella	*sus bananas*	*las suyos*	her bananas
las frutas de ella	*sus frutas*	*las suyas*	her fruit
el gato de nosotros	*nuestro gato*	*el nuestro*	our cat
la historia de nosotros	*nuestra historia*	*la nuestra*	our story
los uniformes de nosotros	*nuestros uniformes*	*los nuestros*	our uniforms
las bufandas de nosotros	*nuestras bufandas*	*las nuestras*	our scarves
el dinero de vosotros	*vuestro dinero*	*el vuestro*	your money
la sala de vosotros	*vuestra sala*	*la vuestra*	your livingroom
los chismes de vosotros	*vuestros chismes*	*los vuestros*	your gossip
las joyas de vosotros	*vuestras joyas*	*las vuestras*	your jewelry
el cuarto de ustedes	*su cuarto*	*el suyo*	your room
la cocina de ustedes	*su cocina*	*la suya*	your kitchen
los regalos de ustedes	*sus regalos*	*los suyos*	your presents
las tazas de ustedes	*sus tazas*	*las suyas*	your cups
el apartamento de ellos	*su apartamento*	*el suyo*	their apartment
la ropa de ellos	*su ropa*	*la suya*	their clothes
los edificios de ellos	*sus edificios*	*los suyos*	their buildings
las cortinas de ellos	*sus cortinas*	*las suyas*	their curtains

This, That, and the Other

Demonstratives are generally used to refer to something by pointing to it, either literally or physically:

Esta casa es mía.

This house is mine.

Ésta es tuya.

This is yours.

In the first example, the demonstrative *esta* is used as an adjective, describing *casa*. In the second example, *ésta* is used as a pronoun, which has replaced the noun phrase *esta casa*. In Spanish, demonstratives used as pronouns carry an accent mark to distinguish them from demonstrative adjectives.

In English, there are two sets of demonstratives: "this" and "these" are used to refer to things near the speaker; "that" and "those" are used for objects far from the speaker. In Spanish, there are three levels of demonstratives:

1. When the object is near the speaker, use *este, esta, estos, estas, éste, ésta, éstos,* or *éstas.*
2. When the object is near the person spoken to, use *ese, esa, esos, esas, ése, ésa, ésos,* or *ésas.*
3. When the object is not near the speaker or near the person spoken to, use *aquel, aquella, aquellos, aquellas, aquél, aquélla, aquéllos,* or *aquéllas.*

In all three forms, demonstratives must agree in number and gender with the object they describe or refer to:

Este restaurante es bueno. Éste es bueno.

This restaurant is good. This one is good.

Esa canción es bonita. Ésa es bonita.

That song is pretty. That one is pretty.

Aquellos chicos son interesantes. Aquéllos son interesantes.

Those guys are interesting. Those ones are interesting.

Definitely Indefinite

Another set of pronouns, which may also be used as adjectives or adverbs, are the indefinite pronouns. Indefinite pronouns are used to refer to nouns in terms of their quantity or order. Some of these pronouns only have one form; others exist only in singular or plural form but change according to gender; yet others must agree in both number and gender with the noun they modify or replace.

Most indefinite pronouns that only have one form are singular in number:

todo	everything
algo	something
nada	nothing
alguien	someone
nadie	no one
mucho	a lot
poco	a little

However, there are two pronouns that are plural: *demás* (the rest) and *todos* (everybody).

Another group of indefinite pronouns indicates gender but only exists in the plural:

varios, varias	various
ambos, ambas	both

The rest of the indefinite pronouns are generally used as adjectives and should agree in number and gender with the noun they modify:

todo, toda, todos, todas	all
mucho, mucha, muchos, muchas	many, much
poco, poca, pocos, pocas	few, little
otro, otra, otros, otras	other
algún, alguna, algunos, algunas	some
ningún, ninguna, ningunos, ningunas	none
quienquier, quienquiera, quienesquiera	whoever
cualquier, cualquiera, cualesquier, cualesquiera	whichever

ESSENTIAL

Words like *mucho* and *poco* may be used to replace nouns (in which case they don't need to follow rules of agreement) or as adjectives (in which case they do need to agree with the noun they modify). In English, these words have different translation depending on their use. Compare: a lot and much/many; a little and few/little.

Practice Makes Perfect

Provide the right subject pronouns in Spanish:

1. the boys __________
2. you (informal) and I __________
3. you (formal) and I __________
4. *Elena, Marta, Diana, y Martín* __________

5. two of you (informal) ____________
6. *el primo* ____________

Choose the right form of address *(tú, usted, vosotros, ustedes)* for each person:

1. *el profesor de matemáticas* ____________
2. *tus amigos* ____________
3. *tu hermana menor* ____________
4. *tus abuelos* ____________
5. *una mujer en la calle* ____________
6. *los lectores de tu escritura* ____________

Fill in the correct direct object pronoun:

1. *Tú compraste una minifalda linda.*

   Tú ____________ *compraste.*
2. *Ellos están buscando a sus tíos.*

   Ellos ____________ *están buscando.*
3. *Veo a ustedes desde la ventana.*

   ____________ *veo desde la ventana.*
4. *Ella encontró a nosotros en el bar.*

   Ella ____________ *encontró en el bar.*

Fill in the correct indirect object pronoun:

1. *El doctor* ____________ *tapó a Mariano las rodillas.*
2. *Nuestra tía* ____________ *regaló a nosotros muchos juguetes.*
3. *Nosotros* ____________ *decimos a ustedes la verdad.*

4. *Mi mamá* ______________ *dijo a mí que debo estudiar muy bien.*

Fill in the correct possessive pronoun:

1. Los llaves de Elena son ______________*llaves*.
2. *El coche mío es* ______________*coche.*
3. *Los estudios de nosotros son* ______________*estudios.*
4. *El cuarto tuyo es* ______________*cuarto.*
5. *El dibujo de Mario es* ______________*dibujo.*
6. *Los proyectos de Antonio y Selena son* ______________ *proyectos.*

To check your answers, refer to the answer key in Appendix D.

CHAPTER 6
Adjectives and Adverbs

ADJECTIVES AND ADVERBS are parts of speech that modify (or describe) other parts of speech and don't have meaning on their own. Adjectives modify nouns; qualifying adjectives (adjetivos calificativos) describe the noun's qualities and traits; and determinant adjectives (adjetivos determinativos) signal the noun's number, order, or location (determinant adjectives are identical to determinant pronouns, except in the way they are used in the sentence). Adverbs have four possible roles: an adverb may be used to modify a verb, an adjective, another adverb, or a verbal phrase.

In Agreement

Adjectives must agree with the nouns they modify. When you learn a new adjective as a vocabulary word, you'll see it presented in the masculine/singular form. Additionally, most adjectives have a plural form, and many have feminine/singular and feminine/plural endings as well.

Frequently, an adjective's masculine/singular form will end in –o. If such is the case, its three other forms are –a, –os, and –as. Take a look at the adjective *rojo* as an example:

cabello rojo	red hair
chaqueta roja	red jacket
labios rojos	red lips
medias rojas	red socks

Almost all other adjectives end with a consonant or –e. These adjectives generally don't change to reflect gender—that is, they only have two forms: singular and plural. The plural form is constructed by adding –es to adjectives that end in consonant and –s to adjectives that end in –e:

el pasto verde	the green pasture
la almohada verde	the green pillow
los camiones verdes	the green trucks
las céspedes verdes	the green lawns
el cielo azul	the blue sky
la pared azul	the blue wall
los ojos azules	the blue eyes
las velas azules	the blue candles

Don't forget that adding –es in the plural may necessitate a change in the use of accent marks or a spelling modification. One common change occurs with adjectives that end –z. Because sounds "ze" and "zi" almost never occur in Spanish, the spelling is modified to –ces to reflect correct pronunciation:

la información veraz	the correct information
las informaciones veraces	(sets of) correct information

A Few Exceptions

Although the majority of adjectives behave according to the few simple rules described here, a few exceptions do exist. Some adjectives end in –a regardless of whether they modify a feminine or a masculine noun, and therefore only have two forms. This is especially true of adjectives that end with –ista, –asta, and –ita (though not when the ending –ita is used to signal a feminine diminutive):

el pensamiento optimista	optimistic thought
el aficionado entusiasta	enthusiastic fan
el ambiente cosmopolita	cosmopolitan environment

As you can see, adjectives *optimista, entusiasta*, and *cosmopolita* end in –a even when they modify masculine nouns like *pensamiento, aficionado*, and *ambiente*. In the plural, the ending would be –as:

los pensamientos optimistas	optimistic thoughts
los aficionados entusiastas	enthusiastic fans
los ambientes cosmopolitas	cosmopolitan environments

FACT

A past participle is a verb form ending in *–ado* (–AR verbs) and *–ido* (–ER and –IR verbs) used in compound tenses: *he comprado* (I have bought), *había vendido* (I had sold). In Spanish, past participles are frequently used as adjectives: *las cosas vendidas* (the sold things). When used as an adjective, the past participle must agree in number and gender with the noun it modifies.

Another set of adjectives make up an exception to the rule that adjectives ending with a consonant only have two forms. In fact, adjectives that end in *–dor*, *–ón*, *–ín*, and *–án* actually have four forms:

vistazo acusador	accusing glance
mirada acusadora	accusing look
vistazos acusadores	accusing glances
miradas acusadoras	accusing looks

obrero holgazán	lazy worker

empleada holgazana	lazy employee
obreros holgazanes	lazy workers
empleadas holgazanas	lazy employees

The correct endings here are –a (feminine/singular), –es (masculine/plural), and –as (feminine/plural).

Switching Places

In English, adjectives always precede the noun they modify, but the same is not necessarily true in Spanish. Generally, qualifying adjectives come after the noun and determinant adjectives appear before the noun:

cosas bonitas	pretty things (qualifying adjective)
otras cosas	other things (determinant adjective)

When a noun is modified by two kinds of adjectives, each adjective will stay in its designated place:

otras cosas bonitas	other pretty things

If both adjectives are qualifying adjectives, the two are connected with *y* (and):

cosas raras y bonitas	rare and pretty things

However, if you wish to emphasize one of the adjectives, drop the *y* and place the more important adjective last:

cosas raras bonitas	rare things that are pretty
cosas bonitas raras	pretty things that are rare

Moving It Up

Sometimes a qualifying adjective may be moved to precede the noun it modifies. This is often the case when the adjective points to an inherent or obvious characteristic and may be thought of as part of a noun phrase, and it doesn't add any new information to the phrase:

el caliente sol	the hot sun
el triste lamento	the sad lament

 **ESSENTIAL**

The following adjectives drop the final –o when they appear before the noun in the masculine/singular form: *bueno/buen* (good), *malo/mal* (bad), *primero/primer* (first), *tercero/tercer* (third), *alguno/algún* (some), *ninguno/ningún* (neither), *grande/gran* (big, great) *cualquiera/cualquier* (whichever).

However, if you wished to emphasize how hot the sun is or how sad the lament, you would move the adjective to the end: *el sol caliente, el lamento triste.* Adjectives indicating subjective judgment or describing abstract nouns may also be moved to precede the noun. This is especially true of *bueno, malo, mejor, peor, grande,* and *pequeño*:

el pequeño pueblo	the small town
la mala suerte	bad luck

Some adjectives will have a slightly different meaning based on their location in relation to the noun. Eventually, you'll be able to sense the difference in meaning, but for now it might be useful to commit the following examples to memory:

adjective	before the noun	after the noun
antiguo	former	ancient
cierto	some	true, certain
diferente(s)	various	different
gran(de)	great	big
medio	half	average
mismo	same	himself, itself
nuevo	new (another)	new (brand new)
pobre	poor (unlucky)	poor (without money)
puro	nothing but, just	pure
simple	just, simply	simple
único	only	unique

Adjectives of Nationality

One important subset of adjectives are the adjectives of nationality. These adjectives are formed from country names. Note that only adjectives that end in –a, –e, and –i in the masculine/singular form have two forms (singular and plural). The rest have four forms: add –a to feminine/singular adjectives, –os to masculine/plural, and –as to feminine/plural forms.

country	adjective of nationality	English
Alemania	*alemán*	German
Argelia	*argelino*	Algerian
Argentina	*argentino*	Argentinean
Australia	*australiano*	Australian
Austria	*austríaco*	Austrian
Bélgica	*belga*	Belgian
Bolivia	*boliviano*	Bolivian

country	adjective of nationality	English
Brasil	*brasileño*	Brazilian
Canadá	*canadiense*	Canadian
Chile	*chileno*	Chilean
China	*chino*	Chinese
Colombia	*colombiano*	Colombian
Corea	*coreano*	Korean
Costa Rica	*costarricense*	Costa Rican
Cuba	*cubano*	Cuban
Dinamarca	*danés*	Danish
Ecuador	*ecuatoriano*	Ecuadorian
Egipto	*egipcio*	Egyptian
Escocia	*escocés*	Scottish
España	*español*	Spanish
Estados Unidos	*estadounidense*	American
Finlandia	*finlandés*	Finnish
Francia	*francés*	French
Grecia	*griego*	Greek
Guatemala	*guatemalteco*	Guatemalan
Haití	*haitiano*	Haitian
Holanda	*holandés*	Dutch
Honduras	*hondureño*	Honduran
Hungría	*húngaro*	Hungarian
India	*indio, hindú*	Indian
Inglaterra	*inglés*	English
Iraq	*iraquí*	Iraqi
Irán	*iraní*	Iranian
Irlanda	*irlandés*	Irish
Israel	*israelí*	Israeli
Japón	*japonés*	Japanese

country	adjective of nationality	English
Líbano	*libanés*	Lebanese
Marruecos	*marroquí*	Moroccan
México	*mexicano*	Mexican
Nicaragua	*nicaragüense*	Nicaraguan
Noruega	*noruego*	Norwegian
Nueva Zelanda	*neocelandés*	New Zealander
Panamá	*panameño*	Panamanian
Paraguay	*paraguayo*	Paraguayan
Perú	*peruano*	Peruvian
Polonia	*polaco*	Polish
Portugal	*portugués*	Portuguese
Puerto Rico	*puertorriqueño*	Puerto Rican
República Dominicana	*dominicano*	Dominican
Rusia	*ruso*	Russian
El Salvador	*salvadoreño*	Salvadoran
Sudán	*sudanés*	Sudanese
Suecia	*sueco*	Swedish
Suiza	*suizo*	Swiss
Tailandia	*tailandés*	Thai
Taiwán	*taiwanés*	Taiwanese
Turquía	*turco*	Turkish
Uruguay	*uruguayo*	Uruguayan
Venezuela	*venezolano*	Venezuelan
Vietnám	*vietnamita*	Vietnamese

Making Comparisons

Adjectives in English as well as in Spanish may be presented in the comparative form. The following constructions may be used to indicate adjectival comparison:

más + adjective + *que*	more + adjective + than
menos + adjective + *que*	less + adjective + than
tan + adjective + *como*	as + adjective + as

Mi hermana es más simpática que la tuya.

My sister is nicer than yours.

Esta película es menos interesante que la de ayer.

This movie is less interesting than the one from yesterday.

Las frutas en el almacén no son tan frescas como en el mercado.

The fruit at the grocery store aren't as fresh as at the market.

In addition to these three constructions, you can use *mejor/mejores* (better), *peor/peores* (worse), *mayor/mayores* (older), and *menor/menores* (younger):

Las obras de Shakespeare son mejores que muchas obras modernas.

Shakespeare's plays are better than many modern plays.

Mi escritura es peor que la suya.

My handwriting is worse than hers.

Todos mis primos son mayores que yo.

All of my cousins are older than me.

Su gerente es menor que él.

His manager is younger than him.

From Best to Worst

In addition to comparative forms, English also has a superlative form: compare "better" and "best," "more" and "most," "higher" and "highest," and so on. Only longer English adjectives require use of another word: "more interesting" and "most interesting," "more frequent" and "most frequent."

In Spanish, all adjectives require the use of *más* (most) and *menos* (least):

Tengo el amigo más amable del mundo.

I have the nicest friend in the world.

Ella es la pintora menos talentosa de la universidad.

She is the least talented painter in the university.

Forming Adverbs

Now that you understand adjectives, let's go on to adverbs. Actually, a few Spanish adjectives also act as adverbs. For example, take a look at how the word *mejor* can be used in both capacities:

la mejor estudiante	the best student
estudiar mejor	to study better

In the first example, *mejor* is an adjective modifying the noun *estudiante*. In the second example, *mejor* is an adverb that modifies the verb *estudiar*. The adjective *peor* (worse) works the same way.

Other adjectives become adverbs with the addition of suffix *-mente* to the feminine singular form. (In English, we have a similar construction that works by adding the suffix –ly to the adjective.)

feminine/singular form	adverb
dudosa (doubtful)	*dudosamente* (doubtfully)
triste (sad)	*tristemente* (sadly)
maravillosa (wonderful)	*maravillosamente* (wonderfully)
fuerte (strong)	*fuertemente* (strongly)
feliz (happy)	*felizmente* (happily)

However, not all adverbs work in this way. There are quite a few you will have to memorize.

ESSENTIAL

When more than one adverb that ends in *–mente* is used to modify a single verb, the suffix is only used on the last adverb of the series. For example: *Te estoy escuchando atenta, abierta, y cuidadosamente.* (I'm listening to you attentively, openly, and carefully.)

How Adverbs Are Used

As its name suggests, an adverb may be used to modify a verb:

Ellos trabajan mucho.

They work a lot.

In this example, the adverb *mucho* modifies the verb *trabajan*—that is, it clarifies how "they" work, how the action of the verb is carried out. Adverbs also modify adjectives:

Ellos son estudiantes muy trabajadores.

They are very hardworking students.

In this example, the adverb *muy* modifies the adjective *trabajadores,* specifying exactly how hardworking the students are. Thirdly, adverbs modify other adverbs:

Ellos trabajan muy bien.

They work very well.

In this example, both *muy* and *bien* are adverbs. *Bien* modifies *trabajan,* because it describes how "they" work; *muy* modifies *bien,* because it describes how well the work is being done.

And that's not all. One other application of the adverb is to modify an entire verb phrase:

Probablemente ellos trabajan en la fábrica.

They probably work at the factory.

In the last example, *probablemente* is an adverb that modifies the verb phrase *trabajan en la fábrica.*

Seven Adverbial Categories

You know how adverbs work, but can you recognize them? If you're having trouble, see if a word fits into one of the following seven categories:

1. Adverbs of place: *alrededor* (around), *cerca* (close), *adentro* (inside)
2. Adverbs of time: *antes* (before), *temprano* (early), *ya* (already, now)
3. Adverbs of manner: *mejor* (better), *estupendamente* (stupendously), *tal* (such)
4. Adverbs of quantity: *bastante* (enough), *tanto* (so much), *muy* (very)
5. Positive adverbs: *sí* (yes), *también* (too), *verdaderamente* (really)

6. Negative adverbs: *no* (no), *tampoco* (neither), *de ninguna manera* (no way)
7. Adverbs of doubt: *quizá* (maybe), *posiblemente* (possibly), *tal vez* (maybe)

Practice Makes Perfect

For each of the following nouns, add an appropriate adjective:

1. *las naranjas* ________________
2. *los libros* ________________
3. *la chica* ________________
4. *las estrellas* ________________
5. *la ropa* ________________
6. *el café* ________________

Combine the adjective and noun in the right order:

1. *bueno + idea* ________________
2. *interesante + cuento* ________________
3. *equivocado + opinión* ________________
4. *pequeño + perritos* ________________
5. *tercero + intento* ________________
6. *rojo + bufandas* ________________

Fill in the blanks with the right adjective of nationality.

1. *Dirk es de Alemania.*

   Es ________________________________.
2. *Fabrizio y Kachina son del Brasil.*

   Son ________________________________.

3. *Patrick es del Canadá.*

   Es __________________________________ .

4. *María es de Chile.*

   Es __________________________________ .

5. *Daniel y Carlos son de Costa Rica.*

   Son __________________________________ .

6. *Aziza es de Egipto.*

   Es __________________________________ .

7. *Kathryn y Janet son de los Estados Unidos.*

   Son __________________________________ .

8. *Michel es de Francia.*

   Es __________________________________ .

Turn the following adjectives into adverbs:

1. *rápido* ________________
2. *feliz* ________________
3. *lento* ________________
4. *triste* ________________
5. *atento* ________________

To check your answers, refer to the answer key in Appendix D.

CHAPTER 7

Introducing the Verb

THE VERB IS ARGUABLY the most important part of the sentence. In fact, many Spanish verbs can form a complete sentence all by themselves: *¡Siéntate!* (Sit down!) *Caminan.* (They are walking.)

Spanish verbs contain much more information in their endings than English verbs, but the flipside is that there are many more endings to choose from. This is why many non-native students have difficulty mastering Spanish verbs. In English, there are just a few basic forms and endings, like the –ed ending to represent past tense. In Spanish, each verb has as many as 106 forms.

Fortunately, verb conjugations follow a set of rules with only a few exceptions, so being able to conjugate many verbs doesn't actually involve memorizing conjugations for each one separately.

Action or State of Being

A verb is a part of speech that refers to the action or state of the subject—what the subject does, what is happening to it, or what it is. In addition to meaning, which remains in the stem (or root) of the verb, the verb is conjugated according to its person, number, voice, mood, tense, and aspect. For example, the verbs *discutir, discutirán,* and *discutan* all carry the inherent meaning of "discussing," but each of the endings carries additional information about the verb and how it acts together with the subject.

In Person

Spanish verbs may appear in one of three grammatical persons. The first person represents the speaker, the second person the addressee, and the third person the object of speech.

I. *yo* (I), *nosotros* (we), *nosotras* (we, feminine)

II. *tú* (you, informal), *vosotros* (you, informal/plural), *vosotras* (you, informal/plural/feminine)

III. *él* (he), *ella* (she), *ello* (it), *ellos* (they), *ellas* (they, feminine).

English grammar works the same way—we also have three persons—but our verbs rarely change form accordingly. The one exception is the verb "to be." In the present tense, its forms are "am," "are," and "is," depending on the person (and number, explained next).

ALERT

Although *usted* and *ustedes,* the two formal "you" pronouns, represent the person spoken to and should theoretically be second person pronouns, they are actually used with third-person verbs. The reason goes back to the original meaning of these words, *vuestra merced* and *vuestras mercedes,* which are third-person nouns.

Singular and Plural

Verbs are also conjugated according to number:

1. **Singular:** *yo, tú, él, ella, ello,* and *usted*
2. **Plural:** *nosotros, nosotras, vosotros, vosotras, ellos, ellas,* and *ustedes*

Together, person and number form the six basic forms of the verb within each tense. In this book (as in many others), conjugations will be presented as follows:

first person/singular	first person/plural
second person/singular	second person/plural
third person/singular	third person/plural

This way, if you need the verb in the *tú* form, you'll need to use the second person/singular form. For *ustedes*, the third person/plural is the right form. The same works with subjects that are not expressed as pronouns. *La estudiante* (the student) will take on the third person/singular form; *Marisca y yo* (Marisca and I) the first person/plural form.

Verbal Voice

A verb may be in active voice or passive voice. Active-voice verbs express the action of the subject:

Yo hablo francés. Hablo francés.

I speak French.

Verbs in passive voice express the action done to the subject (in which the subject is passive):

En Quebec se habla francés.

French is spoken in Quebec. (In Quebec, people speak French.)

How passive voice works in Spanish is covered in greater detail in Chapter 9.

In the Mood

Spanish verbs are also conjugated by mood. Spanish grammar includes three moods (the same is true in English):

1. **Indicative mood** expresses the way things are: *Trabajo mucho.* (I work a lot.)
2. **Subjunctive mood** expresses possibility or opinion, something that isn't necessarily true but could be: *No quiero que mi hijo trabaje.* (I don't want my son to work.)
3. **Imperative mood** expresses commands and requests: *¡Abre la puerta!* (Open the door!)

ESSENTIAL

Many people don't realize that subjunctive mood does exist in English, even though it is not used frequently. For example, in the phrase "if I were a rich man," the verb "were" is in the subjunctive mood. This is why "were" and not "was" is the correct verb here, even though normally we say "I was" when the phrase is in past tense.

It's About Time

Verbs are also broken down by tense. Most languages have at least three basic tenses—the past, present, and future. Some tenses are simple, which means they are expressed with a one-word verb form. Others are compound tenses: These are made up of a conjugated auxiliary verb like *estar* (to be) or *haber* (to have), and another verb in a particular form (present or past participle):

Estoy cansada.

I'm tired.

¿Has comido?

Have you eaten?

Spanish grammar boasts ten tenses in the indicative mood, six tenses in the subjunctive, and one tense in the imperative.

Verbal Aspects

Finally, Spanish verbs may be subdivided into imperfect and perfect forms. Imperfect forms represent action that is being carried out, while perfect forms represent action that has been completed. In general, this is not an important distinction in Spanish because all simple (one-word) forms are imperfect and all compound forms are perfect. The one exception is the preterite (past) tense: it is a simple form that represents action that has been completed.

In the Infinitive

With so many verb conjugations to choose from, the "generic" form that simply identifies the verb is the infinitive. It is an impersonal form that is used in dictionaries and to talk about the verb without a particular tense or person.

In English, infinitives are verbs that are preceded by the particle "to": to think, to walk, to have. In Spanish, infinitives may be recognized by one of the following three endings: –ar, –er, and –ir. For example, *hablar* (to speak), *vender* (to sell), *vivir* (to live). All Spanish verbs can be classified into one of these three groups, so any particular verb may be referred to as an –ar verb, –er verb, or –ir verb. Each group has its own set of regular endings.

The Present Tense

Generally the first tense students will learn in Spanish class is the present tense (in the indicative mood). In Spanish, this is a versatile tense that can be used in many situations. Most obviously, it may be used to indicate simple present tense, just as in English:

Tomo clases de salsa los viernes.

I take salsa lessons on Fridays.

Hace mucho frío.

It's very cold (outside).

Whereas in English we use the present progressive form (I'm thinking, you're going, etc.) to describe actions that are in the process of being completed now as opposed to in general, in Spanish the simple present tense may be used in both cases:

Cantas bien.

You sing well.

Canto en la lluvia.

I'm singing in the rain.

ESSENTIAL

To talk about something that began in the past but continues to the present, use the expression *hace* + (amount of time) + *que* + (present-tense verb). For example: *Hace tres días que no puedo dormir.* (I haven't been able to sleep for three days.)

The simple present tense in Spanish can also be used to indicate actions that will actually happen in the future, but which are planned in the present:

Venimos a la fiesta a las diez.

We'll come to the party at ten.

(We're coming to the party at ten.)

Voy de compras mañana.

I'm going shopping tomorrow.

Regular Conjugations

To conjugate regular verbs in the present tense, all you need to do is drop the infinitive ending of the verb, and choose the correct ending based on the verb's group (whether it's an -AR, -ER, or -IR verb), person, and number.

–AR Endings		–ER Endings		–IR Endings	
–o	–amos	–o	–emos	–o	–imos
–as	–áis	–es	–éis	–es	–ís
–a	–an	–e	–en	–e	–en

As examples, let's take the verbs *hablar* (to speak), *vender* (to sell), and *vivir* (to live):

(yo) hablo, vendo, vivo

(nosotros, nosotras) hablamos, vendemos, vivimos

(tú) hablas, vendes, vives

(vosotros, vosotras) habláis, vendéis, vivís

(él, ella, usted) habla, vende, vive

(ellos, ellas) hablan, venden, viven

Hablo alemán.

I speak German.

Clarisa vende flores en la calle.

Clarisa sells flowers on the street.

(Clarisa is selling flowers on the street.)

¿Vivís aquí?

Do you live here?

Practice Makes Perfect

Add the correct present-tense conjugation of the regular verbs (in parentheses):

1. *Ellos* ______________ *(hablar) inglés.*
2. *Nosotras* ______________ *(vivir) en Madrid.*
3. *Usted* ______________ *(abrir) la puerta.*
4. *Vosotros* ______________ *(vender) frutas en el mercado.*
5. *Elena* ______________ *(preparar) el desayuno.*
6. *Ustedes* ______________ *(decidir) que hacer.*

Translate into English:

1. *El profesor arregla los papeles.*

   ____

2. *Yo ayudo a mis padres con las tareas de la casa.*

   ____

3. *Nosotros entramos por la puerta de atrás.*

   ____

4. *Ella limpia su casa cada semana.*

5. *Tú necesitas ayuda.*

6. *Ellos queman hojas en el jardín.*

Translate into Spanish:

1. You (informal) dance well.

2. You (plural) wash the dishes.

3. We send letters to our friends.

4. They teach classes in the mornings.

5. I drink a lot of water each day.

6. He watches a movie.

To check your answers, refer to the answer key in Appendix D.

CHAPTER 8

Irregular Present Indicative Forms

WHEN IT COMES TO CONJUGATING Spanish verbs, most will simply follow the basic rules: drop the infinitive ending and add the one appropriate to the verb's subject, tense, and mood. However, there are some verbs that, for one reason or another, do not conform to this simple behavior. We call these verbs irregular verbs. Some verbs are only irregular in a few conjugations, while others reliably refuse to conform in any situation.

Quite a number of verbs are irregular in the present indicative tense, and they deserve a chapter of their own. Verb irregularities in other tenses will be covered in the chapters that introduce those particular tenses.

There Is an Explanation

Sure, there are a few irregular verbs that simply defy explanation. There's no obvious reason to explain why it is that the infinitive form *ir* (to go), turns into *voy* (I go) in the first person singular of the present tense. But exceptions like this are rare among Spanish verbs. More often than not, there's a logical explanation for why a verb cannot behave regularly. Often, this has to do with the verb's pronunciation or spelling.

One explanation for irregular verbs that defy explanation is their Latin origin. Whereas most verbs evolved along with the Spanish language, a few retained their old forms that seem irregular to students of modern Spanish.

Retaining Correct Pronunciation

One common irregularity that is actually fairly regular is a change in spelling to make sure the pronunciation remains the same. If this sounds like a paradox, pay attention. Take the words "mice" and "cold" in English. The letter "c" changes its pronunciation depending on the letter that follows it. It's pronounced like "s" before "e," "i," and "y," and like "k" in all other instances. The same is true of "g"—it's pronounced like "dzh" before "e," "i," and "y," and like a hard "g" (the "g" in "go") in all other instances.

Spanish has a very similar pattern. "C" follows the same rule before "e" and "i," and so does "g," except that before "e" and "i" it's pronounced as a hard "h." And "z" behaves strangely as well. It does not like to come before "e" or "i" at all. (If this is not obvious to you, it might be a good time to refer to the pronunciation guide in Chapter 3.)

This presents a problem when a verb's stem ends with a letter like "c," "g," or "z," and an ending that should be added changes the stem's pronunciation. Let's take *coger* (to grab) as an example. The "g" in *coger* is pronounced like a hard "h," and for the verb to be understood, all its conjugations should begin with "cog–" where the "g" retains its pronunciation. However, to form the present indicative *yo* form, "I grab," you need to add the –o ending. In speech, that's easy: the form sounds like "KOH-hoh." When you write it down, however, you encounter an obvious problem: *cogo* spells out "KOH-goh," an entirely different word. Thus, to make the spelling fit with the pronunciation, the verb form undergoes a spelling change: *cojo*. Since "j" retains its pronunciation regardless of what letter follows it, we have to substitute it for the more fickle "g."

ESSENTIAL

Many spelling changes in verb conjugations work along the same principle. Sometimes, though, the explanation might be too complicated, and so you might be told that it's just something you're going to have to memorize.

Making Pronunciation Easier

Another explanation for why some verbs have irregular forms has to do with speech patterns. If a certain verb form is difficult to pronounce, over time it will evolve into an irregular pronunciation. In English, "ain't" might eventually overcome its slang status and become a "real" word. And other words that were formerly incorrect have already found their place in the English dictionary. The same is true in Spanish and most often occurs in the pronunciation of vowels.

One common change is the result of a syllable containing "e" or "o" taking on the accent. To understand what this means, take *pensar* (to think) as an example. In the infinitive form, pronounced pehn-SAHR, the first "e" is not accented. But when adding the endings, the accent does fall on it in four out of six conjugations. If *pensar* were regular, its present indicative conjugations would be as follows:

penso (PEHN-soh)	*pensamos* (pehn-SAH-mohs)
pensas (PEHN-sahs)	*pensáis* (pehn-SAis)
pensa (PEHN-sah)	*pensan* (PEHN-sahn)

However, because of a tendency in Spanish to modify an accented "e" to "ie" or "i," the correct forms are:

pienso (PIEHN-soh)	*pensamos* (pehn-SAH-mohs)
piensas (PIEHN-sahs)	*pensáis* (pehn-SAis)
piensa (PEHN-sah)	*piensan* (PIEHN-sahn)

Unless you are a native speaker and these forms come naturally to you, you won't necessarily know which verbs follow this pronunciation change. However, once you learn that a particular verb belongs to a group of "e > ie" verbs, you'll know it'll behave just as *pensar* in present indicative tense.

ALERT

Pronunciation change also works with consonants. For example, a group of verbs with a stem ending in "n" like *tener* (to have) and *venir* (to come) gain a "g" at the end of the stem in the *yo* form of the present indicative. This means that instead of *yo teno* and *yo veno,* the correct forms are *yo tengo* and *yo vengo.*

Spelling Change Verbs

A change in spelling to reflect correct pronunciation is one of the most common irregularities found in Spanish verbs, and the one that generally makes sense. Spelling changes happen to "tricky" letters like *c* and *g,* which have more than one pronunciation depending on the letter that follows, and vowel combinations like *ui.*

From "I" to "Y"

In verbs that end in –uir, the long "i" sound is retained in all six conjugations, which requires changing the spelling of some of the forms from "i" to "y." Take a look at the conjugations of *influir* (to influence) and *huir* (to flee):

influyo	*influimos*
influyes	*influís*
influye	*influyen*

huyo	*huimos*
huyes	*huís*
huye	*huyen*

Other verbs that follow the same pattern are *atribuir* (to attribute), *concluir* (to conclude), *destruir* (to destroy), *incluir* (to include), and *sustituir* (to substitute).

ESSENTIAL

As you continue learning irregular verbs in present indicative tense, you'll probably notice that many of them follow the same change in four out of six conjugations—*nosotros* and *vosotros* forms are the ones that remain regular. The explanation is simple: only these two forms have accented endings (AH-mohs, EH-mohs, EE-mohs and AH-is, EH-is, EES).

The Inconstant "C"

Many verbs undergo a spelling change because their stem ends with a "c," which needs to maintain its pronunciation, either as "s" or "k". For example, verbs that end in –ecer maintain the "s" sound at the end of the stem. This works just fine with most forms of the present indicative, but poses a problem in the *yo* form.

Take *aparecer* (to appear) as an example. If you simply add the –o ending, the result will be *apareco,* with the "c" pronounced as "k." And *apareso* doesn't work either (in Spain, the "c" in *aparecer* is pronounced "th," so "s" wouldn't serve as a substitution). Instead, both spelling and pronunciation change a bit, from "c" to "zc": *aparezco*. Take a look at the conjugations of *aparecer* and *establecer* (to establish):

aparezco	*aparecemos*
apareces	*aparecéis*
aparece	*aparecen*

establezco	*establecemos*
estableces	*establecéis*
establece	*establecen*

Other -ecer verbs that undergo a "c > zc" change in the *yo* form are *agradecer* (to thank), *conocer* (to know), *crecer* (to grow), *merecer* (to deserve), *obedecer* (to obey), *ofrecer* (to offer), *parecer* (to seem), *permanecer* (to remain), and *pertenecer* (to belong).

Verbs that end in -ecer are not the only ones subject to the "c > zc" change; the same is true of verbs that end in -ucir, like *conducir* (to drive) and *traducir* (to translate). Note that these are -ir verbs, which means they have different endings:

conduzco	*conducimos*
conduces	*conducís*
conduce	*conducen*

traduzco	*traducimos*
traduces	*traducís*
traduce	*traducen*

Other -ucir verbs that work in the exactly the same way are *lucir* (to shine) and *producir* (to produce).

When the Verb Stem Ends in "G"

Verbs that need to retain the hard "h" sound of the "g" at the end of the stem undergo a "g > j" change in the *yo* form of the present indicative, to retain the correct pronunciation with the ending –o. This is true of all verbs ending in –ger or –gir, like *proteger* (to protect) and *dirigir* (to direct). Again, notice that the endings still reflect the differences between –er and –ir verbs.

protejo	*protegemos*
proteges	*protegéis*
protege	*protegen*

dirijo	*dirigimos*
diriges	*dirigís*
dirige	*dirigen*

Other –ger and –gir verbs that undergo the same change in the *yo* form are *afligir* (to afflict), *coger* (to grab), *encoger* (to shrink), *exigir* (to demand), *fingir* (to pretend), and *recoger* (to gather).

FACT

In verbs that end with –guir, the "g" remains in place, but another change takes place: In the *yo* form, the stem drops the "u" along with the "ir," so *extinguir* (to extinguish) becomes *extingo* and *seguir* (to follow) becomes *sigo*. *Seguir* has another irregularity as well—the vowel change in the stem (e > i), described later in this chapter.

Use of Accent Marks

Some spelling irregularities are pretty simple: They involve a change in the use of accent marks. For example, many verbs that end in –iar require an accent mark over the "í" in four of the present indicative conjugations (these four are the usual suspects—all singular forms and third person plural). Take a look at *confiar* (to confide) and *espiar* (to spy), as two examples:

confío	*confiamos*
confías	*confiáis*
confía	*confían*

espío	*espiamos*
espías	*espiáis*
espía	*espían*

Other verbs that require an accent mark over the "í" are *enviar* (to send), *guiar* (to guide) and *variar* (to vary).

The same pattern also applies to –uar verbs, except it's the "ú" that requires the accent mark. This change occurs with the verbs *actuar* (to act) and *continuar* (to continue):

actúo	*actuamos*
actúas	*actuáis*
actúa	*actúan*

continúo	*continuamos*
continúas	*continuáis*
continúa	*continúan*

Changes in Pronunciation

As you've seen so far, the need to retain regular pronunciation may result in a spelling change irregularity. However, some verb conjugations simply change in pronunciation. In the present indicative, verbs are most likely to undergo a pronunciation change in the *yo* form, which has to do with its –o ending.

One common change is the addition of "g" in verbs like *hacer* (to do) and *salir* (to leave):

hago	*hacemos*
haces	*hacéis*
hace	*hacen*

salgo	*salimos*
sales	*salís*
sale	*salen*

ALERT

Adding a prefix to a verb generally won't change its behavior in terms of its endings. For example, *distraigo* (I distract) and *atraigo* (I attract) behave the same as *traigo* (I bring).

The following table includes other verbs that take on a "g" in the *yo* form:

caer	*caigo*	I fall
decir	*digo*	I say
oír	*oigo*	I hear
poner	*pongo*	I put
tener	*tengo*	I have
traer	*traigo*	I bring
valer	*valgo*	I cost
venir	*vengo*	I come

Not all of these verbs are regular in the other five conjugations of the present indicative. For example, *tener* and *venir* are also stem-change verbs (described in the next section).

In addition to the *yo* forms that need an extra "g," a few verbs have *yo* conjugations that are irregular and don't follow any particular pattern:

caber	*quepo*	I fit
dar	*doy*	I give
saber	*sé*	I know
ver	*veo*	I see

Stem Changing Verbs

Some groups of Spanish verbs undergo a stem change, that is, their stem or root changes spelling and pronunciation in four of the six conjugation forms (excluding *nosotros* and *vosotros*). The most common changes occur in the stem's vowel: "e" may change to "ie" or "i," and "o" may change to "ue" or "u."

The Unstable "E"

A number of –ar and –er verbs undergo an "e > ie" change in the stem when the "e" is in the accented syllable. Take a look at the conjugations of the verbs *apretar* (to grip) and *defender* (to defend):

aprieto	*apretamos*
aprietas	*apretáis*
aprieta	*aprietan*

defiendo	*defendemos*
defiendes	*defendéis*
defiende	*defienden*

Other verbs that follow the same pattern are worth memorizing:

atravesar	*atravieso*	I cross
cerrar	*cierro*	I close
comenzar	*comienzo*	I commence
empezar	*empiezo*	I begin
encender	*enciendo*	I light
gobernar	*gobierno*	I govern
pensar	*pienso*	I think
perder	*pierdo*	I lose
querer	*quiero*	I want
sentar	*siento*	I sit down

The verb *tener* (to have) is also an "e > ie" verb, with an additional irregularity in the *yo* form:

tengo	*tenemos*
tienes	*tenéis*
tiene	*tienen*

A similar modification occurs with –ir verbs as well. In the conjugations where the "e" is accented, it is replaced with "i." Take a look at the verbs *gemir* (to moan) and *repetir* (to repeat) as examples:

gimo	*gemimos*
gimes	*gemís*
gime	*gimen*

repito	*repetimos*
repites	*repetís*
repite	*repiten*

Other verbs in this category are *medir* (to measure), *pedir* (to ask), *seguir* (to follow), *servir* (to serve), and *vestir* (to dress).

ESSENTIAL

The stem-change rule is generally different for –ar/–er and –ir verbs. The –ar and –er verbs undergo a "e > ie" change; –ir verbs undergo a "e > i" change. However, a few –ir verbs do have an "e > ie" stem change: *mentir* > *miente* (he lies), *preferir* > *prefiere* (he prefers), *sentir* > *siente* (he feels), and *venir* > *viene* (he comes).

When "O" Is under Stress

Just as stressed "e" may undergo a change to "i" or "ie," a stressed "o" in some irregular verbs changes to "u" or "ue." In the present indicative, the change is limited to "o > ue." Take a look at two examples: *almorzar* (to have lunch) and *dormir* (to sleep):

almuerzo	*almorzamos*
almuerzan	*almorzáis*
almuerza	*almuerzan*

duermo	*dormimos*
duermes	*dormís*
duerme	*duermen*

Other verbs that follow the "o > ue" stem change include the following:

contar	*cuento*	I tell
costar	*cuesto*	I cost
doler	*duelo*	I hurt
jugar	*juego*	I play
morir	*muero*	I die
mostrar	*muestro*	I show
poder	*puedo*	I can
recordar	*recuerdo*	I remember
volar	*vuelo*	I fly
volver	*vuelvo*	I return

Just Plain Irregular

Irregular verbs reviewed so far share their irregularity with at least a few other verbs. But there are some verbs that have unique irregularities. All you can do with these verbs is memorize their conjugations. The following tables include conjugations of *haber* (to have), *ir* (to go), *oler* (to smell), and *reír* (to laugh). Note that *haber* and *ir* will be covered in greater detail in subsequent chapters. And we'll take a look at two more irregular verbs, *ser* and *estar*, both translated as "to be," in the next section.

he	*hemos*
has	*habéis*
ha	*han*

voy	*vamos*
vas	*vais*
va	*van*

huelo	*olemos*
hueles	*oléis*
huele	*huelen*

río	*reímos*
ríes	*reís*
ríe	*ríen*

Ser Versus *Estar*

Spanish has two verbs that may be translated as "to be"—*ser* and *estar*. Both have irregular conjugations; the verb *ser* is particularly unusual:

soy	*somos*
eres	*sois*
es	*son*

estoy	*estamos*
estás	*estáis*
está	*están*

Because both *ser* and *estar* have only one equivalent translation in English, many students of Spanish have difficulty understanding the difference between the two verbs. A good rule of thumb to get you started is that *ser* describes permanent state and *estar* refers to temporary condition or location.

Permanently *Ser*

Ser means "is" in the sense that something *is* the way it is:

Soy rubia y tú eres morena.

I am blonde and you are a brunette.

Patrizio es de Italia. Es italiano.

Patrizio is from Italy. He is Italian.

Angelina y Alberto son estudiantes.

Angelina and Alberto are students.

Nationality, Religion, and So On

Ser is used to describe nationality; in combination with *de,* it may be used to say where someone is from:

¿Es usted de Chile? Sí, soy de Chile. Soy chilena.

Are you from Chile? Yes, I'm from Chile. I'm Chilean.

It is also used with other permanent characteristics that describe a person's status, such as religion, profession, or family relationship:

Pepe Ortiz es mi abuelo.

Pepe Ortiz is my grandfather.

No todos los mexicanos son católicos.

Not all Mexicans are Catholic.

Somos médicos, pero no somos santos.

We are doctors, but we aren't saints.

Personal Characteristics

Characteristics that don't change from day to day are also described with *ser*. These might be physical features like eye color or height, or personality features, like intelligence or kindness. Features that don't change over a short period of time, such as being young or old, are also described with *ser:*

Mariana es bonita y muy simpática.

Mariana is pretty and very nice.

Ellos son jóvenes.

They are young.

FACT

Ser and *estar* are also used in verbal constructions. *Ser* makes an appearance in the Spanish passive voice, and *estar* combines with a present participle to form the present progressive tense. Both of these constructions are described further in the next chapter.

Indication of Possession

Possessive constructions in Spanish rely on *ser* to establish the relationship between the possessor and the possessed.

La idea no es mía.

The idea isn't mine.

La camiseta blanca es de María.

The white shirt is Maria's.

Over Time

The one exception to the idea of *ser* being used to describe what is permanent is that this verb is employed in expressions of time—to say what day, week, month, and year it is, and also what time it is:

Son las dos de la tarde.

It's two in the afternoon.

Hoy es lunes, ¿verdad?

Today is Monday, right?

On the Move with *Estar*

Estar is often translated as "to be located," but its role is not limited to indicating physical location. *Estar* is also the verb "to be" used to describe temporary characteristics.

On Location

Whereas *ser* may be used to say where you are from, *estar* is the verb of choice when you need to explain where you are, geographically:

Estoy en la cocina.

I'm in the kitchen.

Federico y Ramona están en Perú.

Federico and Ramona are in Peru.

In the Mood

Estar is also used when describing a mood, such as boredom, tiredness, or happiness. It may also be used to describe a temporary condition–being open, closed, accessible, and so on.

Clara está enferma. Le duele la cabeza y tiene fiebre.

Clara is sick. Her head hurts and she has a fever.

Cuando voy a la clase de matemáticas, estoy muy aburrido.

When I go to math class, I am very bored.

¿Cómo están ustedes? Estamos bien.

How are you? We're fine.

Choosing Wisely

One way to understand how *ser* and *estar* differ is by comparing pairs of phrases where the only difference is the verb:

Las chicas son bellas.

The girls are pretty (in general).

Las chicas están bellas.

The girls look pretty (today).

In the first sentence, prettiness is a permanent characteristic of the girls; in the second, it is their condition on a particular occasion. Here is another example:

Nosotros somos aburridos.

We are boring.

Nosotros estamos aburridos.

We are bored.

Again, in the first sentence the adjective reflects a characteristic of the subject, "us." In the second sentence, the adjectives describes the mood or condition of the subject.

Practice Makes Perfect

Conjugate the following irregular verbs (in parentheses) in the present tense:

1. *Los niños ______________ (jugar) en su cuarto.*
2. *Nosotras los ______________ (ver) a ellos desde la ventana.*

3. *¿ __________ (recordar) ustedes lo que deben hacer?*
4. *Tú __________ (cerrar) el libro.*
5. *Vosotros __________ (querer) salir a bailar.*
6. *Ella __________ (contar) chismes todo el tiempo.*
7. *Nosotros __________ (permanecer) aquí.*
8. *Yo les __________ (exigir) a mis padres que me dejen salir.*
9. *Tú __________ (mentir), ¿no es así?*
10. *Vosotros __________ (poder) descansar un rato.*

Fill in *ser* or *estar* and conjugate correctly:

1. *Ella __________ una ladrona.*

   __________ mala.
2. *El Señor Órtiz __________ abogado.*
3. *Mis hijos tienen el pelo negro.*

   __________ morenos.
4. *__________ las once de la noche.*
5. *Tú tienes fiebre.*

   __________ enfermo.
6. *Ustedes __________ muy simpáticos.*
7. *Cuando viajamos juntos, yo __________ muy alegre.*
8. *Yo __________ de México.*

   __________ mexicana.
9. *No __________ bien. Me siento mal.*
10. *¿ __________ usted alegre hoy?*

To check your answers, refer to the answer key in Appendix D.

CHAPTER 9

A Quick Verb Usage Guide

WHEREAS CHAPTER 8 COVERS irregular verb forms, this chapter will turn your attention to irregularities in terms of usage—those tricky verbs that make no sense if all you have is a literal translation. Sometimes knowing the English meaning of something isn't enough. You also need to know how you can apply it in Spanish. From the difference between *saber* and *conocer* (both translated as "to know") to the Spanish passive voice, this chapter covers verbs and verb constructions that may baffle English speakers and native Spanish speakers alike.

Saber or Conocer?

If you don't speak Spanish as a native language, you might have difficulty choosing between *saber* and *conocer.* Both are translated as "to know." *Saber* may also mean "to be able to do," and *conocer* means "to meet," but in some situations the distinction isn't clear. Before we look at each verb more closely, let's review their conjugations in the present indicative:

sé	*sabemos*
sabes	*sabéis*
sabe	saben

conozco	*conocemos*
conoces	*conocéis*
conoce	*conocen*

Abilities and Skills

Saber should be your verb of choice if you are talking about knowing how to do something:

¿Sabes esquiar en las montañas?

Do you know how to ski in the mountains?

Los estudiantes saben matemáticas e inglés, pero todavía no saben castellano.

The students know math and English, but they still don't know Spanish.

ESSENTIAL

Here's a tip to help you remember how to use *saber:* It's related to *sabio* (wise, a wise person) and *sabiduría* (wisdom), words that indicate the learned knowledge as well as inteligence someone possesses.

Saber is also used to express what someone knows:

¿Sabe lo que pasó ayer por la ciudad?

Do you know what happened yesterday in the city?

Yo sé lo que vas a decir.

I know what you're going to say.

It's Who You Know

Conocer is used to express whom you know in the sense of whom you've met. For example, *Valentina conoce a Rodolfo* means "Valentina knows Rodolfo" in the sense that she's met him, not merely that she knows who he is. Similarly, you can use *conocer* to talk about the things that you know and are familiar with, as well as places you've visited:

Conozco los árboles del parque que Selena mencionó en su presentación.

I know the trees from the park that Selena mentioned in her presentation.

¿Conocen la ciudad donde nací?

Do you know the city where I was born?

Note that in the last example, the question is whether you've visited the city, rather than whether you've heard about it.

Talking about the Weather

Verbs associated with talking about the weather serve as a good example of how you can't always rely on direct translation between English and Spanish. In English, we generally use the verb "to be" to describe the weather: It's sunny. It was cold. It will be windy. In Spanish, *estar* may be used in some cases:

¿Cómo está el tiempo?

How is the weather?

Está lloviendo.

It's raining.

Está nublado.

It's cloudy.

Está nevando.

It's snowing.

However, a more common verb is *hacer* (to make):

¿Qué tiempo hace?

Literally, this question may be translated as "What (kind of) weather is made?" But the question is really asking "How is the weather?" Common answers are:

Hace sol.

It's sunny.

Hace mucho frío.

It's very cold.

Hace mucho calor.

It's very hot.

Hace fresco.

It's cool.

Another verb which may be used to talk about the weather is *hay,* described in the next section.

There Is/There Are

"There is" and "there are" are present-tense constructions used in English to describe an object or objects at a particular location. In Spanish, the equivalent expression is *hay.* This form will work whether you are referring to one or more objects:

Hay un pequeño almacén entre el restaurante italiano y la librería.

There is a small grocery store between the Italian restaurant and the bookstore.

Hay muchos libros en el estante.

There are a lot of books on the bookshelf.

The expression will work the same way in other tenses—all you need to do is conjugate *haber* in the third-person singular form of the right tense:

Había un pequeño almacén entre el restaurante italiano y la librería.

There was a small grocery store between the Italian restaurant and the bookstore.

Habrá muchos libros en el estante.

There will be a lot of books on the bookshelf.

 **QUESTION?**

What does *haber* actually mean?
The verb *haber* may be translated as "to have" when it is used in compound tenses: *he hablado* (I have spoken), *había dicho* (she had said). But it doesn't really have a meaning on its own.

Just Finished

In Spanish, you've got the option to talk about something that just has been done with a present indicative form of the verb *acabar* (to finish), a regular –ar verb used with preposition *de*. Here is how it works:

Acabo de cocinar la cena.

I just finished cooking dinner.

Acaban de estudiar para el examen.

They just finished studying for the test.

Without *de*, the verb simply means "to finish" or "to end":

Los exámenes acaban el viernes.

The exams will end on Friday.

Going to Do It with *Ir*

Whereas *acabar de* in the present tense is used to express actions that were just finished, the construction *ir a* in the present tense can be used to talk about things that will happen in the future–things that are going to be done:

Voy a plantar los flores en el jardín.
I'm going to plant the flowers in the garden.

Vamos a buscar a Martín por la playa.
We're going to look for Martin at the beach.

As you can see, *ir a* is equivalent to the English expression "going to." It works almost the same way in Spanish, except that the present indicative form of the verb *ir* is used. Here is how *ir* (to go) is conjugated:

voy	*vamos*
vas	*vais*
va	*van*

Progressive Forms

Progressive tenses are used to show ongoing action. In English, progressive tenses are formed with the verb "to be" and the present participle. The same is true in Spanish–the main verb in Spanish progressive tenses is *estar*. To refresh your memory, here are the conjugations of *estar* in the present indicative:

estoy	*estamos*
estás	*estáis*
está	*están*

The most commonly used progressive is the present progressive tense. In English, we often rely on this tense to talk about things that are going on right now, as opposed to regularly. Compare the following two sentences:

She talks to me. (in general)

She is talking to me. (right now)

In Spanish, even actions that take place "right now" may be described with the present indicative form: *Ella habla conmigo.* However, if you want to highlight the fact that the action is occurring right now (this minute), you can use the present progressive form and say *Ella está hablando conmigo.*

ESSENTIAL

The verb *seguir* (to follow, to continue) is occasionally employed in progressive constructions as well. For example, *sigo hablando* means "I keep on speaking" or "I am speaking."

Forming the Present Participle

Present participle is a verbal form that corresponds to the English form ending in –ing: going, walking, talking, and so on. In Spanish, a present participle is formed by dropping the infinitive ending and adding the correct present participle ending:

verb group	present participle ending	examples
–ar verbs	–ando	*hablando* (speaking)
–er verbs	–iendo	*corriendo* (running)
–ir verbs	–iendo	*viviendo* (living)

Only a few present participles are irregular. If the stem of an –er and –ir verb ends in a vowel, its present participle ending is –yendo:

caer	*cayendo*	falling
creer	*creyendo*	believing
leer	*leyendo*	reading
oír	*oyendo*	hear
traer	*trayendo*	bringing

Present participle forms of –ir verbs also retain the stem change that occurs in the third person singular form of the preterite tense (covered in Chapter 11):

infinitive	preterite	present participle	English
decir	*dijo*	*diciendo*	saying
dormir	*durmió*	*durmiendo*	sleeping
morir	*murió*	*muriendo*	dying
pedir	*pidió*	*pidiendo*	asking
repetir	*repitió*	*repitiendo*	repeating
sentir	*sintió*	*sintiendo*	feeling
servir	*sirvió*	*sirviendo*	serving
venir	*vino*	*viniendo*	coming

The only other irregular forms are *pudiendo* (the present participle form of *poder,* "can") and *yendo* (going).

In Other Tenses

Present progressive is just one of several progressive tenses. In each tense, the present participle remains the same, but the form of *estar* is conjugated differently. In the present progressive, *estar* is conjugated in the present indicative. The rest of the progressives are organized as follows:

progressive form	the conjugation form of estar	example
past progressive	imperfect tense	*estaba hablando* (I was talking)
past progressive	preterite tense	*estuve hablando* (I was talking)
future progressive	future tense	*estaré hablando* (I will be talking)
conditional progressive	conditional tense	*estaría hablando* (I would be talking)

QUESTION?

Why are there two different past-tense progressive forms? If you haven't had an introduction to preterite and imperfect past tenses, you might be confused to see that progressive forms have two different past-tense forms. However, once you learn about these tenses, you'll be able to see the difference in meaning between *estaba hablando* and *estuve hablando.*

Passive Voice

Passive voice makes it possible to drop the subject of the verb from the sentence by putting the object in its place and substituting the active verb with the correct form of *ser* ("to be") and a past participle. To refresh your memory, here's how to conjugate *ser* in the present indicative:

soy	*somos*
eres	*sois*
es	*son*

Passive voice works the same way in English and in Spanish. Here is how to turn an active voice sentence into a passive voice one:

Carlos escribió la carta.

Carlos wrote the letter.

La carta es escrita.

The letter is written.

As you can see, the switch to passive voice makes it possible to have the letter, and not Carlos, as the subject of the sentence, even though it's the object of the verb's action. The "real" subject, Carlos, is dropped from the sentence. It's possible to add Carlos back in, as long as it's in the prepositional phrase with *por* (by):

La carta es escrita por Carlos.

The letter is written by Carlos.

Here's another example:

El trabajo es hecho por Manuel.

The work is done by Manuel.

The Past Participle

To use the passive voice, you need to know how to form a past participle. The past participle is the same form that is used in compound tenses with *haber* (to have): *he comprado* (I have bought); *habrían viviendo* (they would have lived), and so on. In Spanish, the rule for forming the past participle are pretty simple: drop the infinitive ending and add the correct past participle ending.

verb group	present participle ending	examples
–ar verbs	–ado	*hablado* (spoken)
–er verbs	–ido	*perdido* (lost)
–ir verbs	–ido	*vivido* (lived)

The same verbs that are irregular as present participles (–er and –ir verbs with a stem ending in a vowel) are also irregular as past participles. This time, they gain an accent mark over the end-stem vowel:

caer	*caído*	fallen
creer	*creído*	believed
leer	*leído*	read
oír	*oído*	listened
traer	*traído*	brought
Other examples of irregular past participles are:		
abrir	*abierto*	opened
cubrir	*cubierto*	covered
decir	*dicho*	said
escribir	*escrito*	written
hacer	*hecho*	done
ir	*ido*	gone
morir	*muerto*	died
poner	*puesto*	put
romper	*roto*	broken
ser	*sido*	been
ver	*visto*	seen
volver	*vuelto*	returned

Passive voice is rarely used in good writing because you lose the clarity of who performed the action of the verb, but sometimes that's intentional. For example, saying "the vase is broken" is a nicer way of saying that Janet broke the vase.

Whereas the past participle only has one form when it's used in compound tenses, in the passive voice it must agree with the subject of the sentence (that is, the object of the action) in gender and number. Compare:

El asunto es arreglado por el presidente de la companía.

The matter is settled by the company's president.

La cuestión es resuelta por el presidente de la companía.

The question is resolved by the company's president.

Los asuntos son arreglados por el presidente de la companía.

The matters are settled by the company's president.

Las cuestiones son resueltas por el presidente de la companía.

The questions are resolved by the company's president.

Practice Makes Perfect

Fill in *saber* or *conocer*, as appropriate:

1. *Caterina* ____________ *la historia de los Estados Unidos.*
2. *Ellos*________________*a todos en la escuela.*

3. *Nosotros no _________________ qué hacer.*
4. *¿ ______________ (tú) lo que está pasando afuera?*
5. *No ____________ a ese chico.*

Translate into Spanish:

1. She is reading (right now).

____

2. There is a box on the table.

____

3. They are walking (right now).

____

4. (They) speak French in France.

____

5. How is the weather?

____

To check your answers, refer to the answer key in Appendix D.

CHAPTER 10

Object of the Verb

CHAPTER 5 INCLUDED AN OVERVIEW of object and reflexive pronouns: what they are and their English translation. In this chapter, you'll begin learning how pronouns are used together with Spanish verbs.

Object pronouns work a bit differently in Spanish, and many students get confused by all those small words that seem to be sprinkled around a Spanish sentence in abundance. So let's get things straight once and for all. A verb may come with a direct object and/or indirect object, or it may be reflexive and require a reflexive object. Verbs that may use or require one or more of these objects are covered in this chapter.

What Is an Object?

The basic structure of a simple sentence is subject + verb + object. Both the subject and object may be nouns, pronouns, or noun phrases. The difference between the subject and object is that the subject is who or what performs the action, whereas the object is the receiver of the action, whether directly or indirectly.

Prepositional Objects

One common group of objects is prepositional phrases, made up of a preposition, noun (or pronoun), and possibly articles and/or adjectives. Here are a few examples:

Ella suele bailar en la calle.

She usually dances in the street.

Trabajamos desde las siete de la mañana hasta las cuatro de la tarde.

We work from seven in the morning until four in the afternoon.

In these sentences, *bailar en la calle, desde las siete de la mañana,* and *hasta las cuatro de la tarde* are prepositional objects. Simply speaking, they are objects of the verb *suele bailar* and *trabajamos* and happen to include a preposition.

Direct and Indirect Objects

Other objects are not mitigated by the preposition. These are direct and indirect objects. What's the difference between the two? The direct object takes on the action of the verb directly; the indirect object is the person or thing for whom the action is performed. That is, direct object answers the question "whom or what?" whereas the indirect object answers the question "to/for whom or what?" Compare the following two examples:

Limpio la casa.

I clean the house.

Los ayudo a mis padres a limpiar la casa.

I help my parents clean the house.

In the first example, *la casa* is the direct object of the verb *limpio:*

¿Limpio qué? Limpio la casa.

I clean what? I clean the house.

In the second example, *la casa* is still the direct object; the indirect object of the verb phrase *ayudo a limpiar* is *a mis padres,* reinforced by the pronoun *los* (more on this later). Here's how you can check if you're right:

¿Ayudo a limpiar la casa a quién? Los ayudo limpiar la casa a mis padres.

Whom do I help clean the house? I help my parents clean the house.

Transitive and Intransitive Verbs

Verbs that require the presence of a direct object are known as transitive verbs. Some verbs can never appear without a direct object: The phrase *yo miro* (I watch) can't form a complete sentence, because it's necessary to specify the direct object–whom or what I watch. Verbs that need a direct object are called transitive because they form a transition between the subject and the object of the sentence.

FACT

In Spanish, a verb that takes on an indirect object without having a direct object is also considered intransitive. Some verbs may function transitively *or* intransitively, while others always stay in one category.

If a verb functions without a direct object, it is called an intransitive verb: *yo camino* doesn't require a direct object. In fact, it can't. If you want to add more information about the verb, you'll have to add a prepositional phrase:

Yo camino por la orilla del río.

I walk along the banks of the river.

Direct Objects

The direct object is direct because it receives the action "directly"—that is, it follows the verb and is not mediated by a preposition. The direct object may be a part of a phrase, but the rest of the phrase simply modifies the direct object. Here are a few examples of direct objects in a basic Spanish sentence:

Ellos miran la television los domingos.

They watch television on Sundays.

Ellas toman café en el patio.

They are drinking coffee on the patio.

The direct objects here are *la television* and *café:* Television receives the action of being watched, and coffee receives the action of being drunk. As you may remember, direct objects may be represented by direct object pronouns:

Direct Object Pronouns	
singular	**plural**
me (me)	*nos* (us)
te (you, informal)	*os* (you, informal in Spain)
lo, la (you, formal)	*los, las* (you)
lo, la (him, her, it)	*los, las* (them)

Ellos la miran los domingos.

They watch it on Sundays.

Ellas lo toman en el patio.

They are drinking it on the patio.

As you can see from these examples, when the direct object is a pronoun, it moves up to precede the verb.

ALERT

In Spanish, as a general rule, any direct object that represents a person must be introduced with a personal *a.* Compare the two following: *Miro la televisión.* (I watch television.) *Miro a Pablo y Juanita.* (I watch Pablo and Juanita.)

If you've got a compound verb, the direct object pronoun will come before the conjugated form of *haber:*

Ya lo he aprendido.

I have learned it already.

Indirect Objects

The indirect object represents the person (or, less often, object) to whom or for whom the action of the verb is performed. Some indirect objects appear alongside direct objects, while others appear on their own:

Le regalo flores a mi novia cada cumpleaños.

I give flowers to my girlfriend every birthday.

Les pido perdón a Yolanda y su hija.

I ask Yolanda and her daughter for their forgiveness.

Te pregunto. (no direct object)

I am asking you.

Even if the indirect object is represented by a noun, the indirect object pronoun should be added before the verb for emphasis. To review, the following are the indirect object pronouns:

Indirect Object Pronouns	
singular	**plural**
me (me)	*nos* (us)
te (you, informal)	*os* (you, informal in Spain)
le (you, formal)	*les* (you)
le (him, her, it)	*les* (them)

As you may remember, direct and indirect object pronouns are identical in the first and second persons.

ESSENTIAL

If your verb is made up of two parts, an active verb and an infinitive, the object pronoun may come before the verb pair or attached to the infinitive: *Lo necesito llamar. Necesito llamarlo.* (I need to call him.) The same applies to direct, indirect, and reflexive pronouns.

Double Pronouns

If both the direct and indirect object in the sentence are pronouns, they are placed before the verb, and the indirect object pronoun always comes first. Here's the correct order of the sentence:

subject + indirect object pronoun + direct object pronoun + verb

It may take a while for you to get used to this order, but it's not difficult to understand. Here are a few other examples to help you get the hang of it:

Me manda cartas cada semana. Me las manda.

He sends me letters every week. He sends them to me. (To me them he sends.)

Te explico las respuestas mañana. Te las explico.

I'll explain you the answers tomorrow. I'll explain them to you. (To you them I'll explain.)

If both pronouns are in third person, the indirect object pronoun undergoes a change from *le/les* to *se*. The reason for the change is to avoid the awkward combinations like *le lo* or *les la*. Here are a few examples:

Le pago la cuenta al camarero. Se la pago.

I pay the bill (to the waiter). I pay it (to him).

Les doy una sonrisa. Se la doy.

I give them a smile. I give it to them.

A Different Kind of Construction

In Spanish, the indirect object allows us to create a construction that is best exemplified with the verb *gustar* (to like). Compare the Spanish and the English:

Me gustan los dulces.

I like sweets.

In English, the sentence is a standard subject + verb + direct object. In Spanish, though, the role of each word differs:

me (indirect object pronoun) + *gustan* (verb) + *dulces* (subject)

In Spanish, the subject of the sentence is *dulces*, which are liked by me. This is why the verb *gustar* is conjugated in the third person plural. In fact, because the subject is always what is being liked, the verb *gustar* is limited to third-person singular (one thing) or third-person plural (more than one thing). The following table outlines the possible combinations:

singular subject	plural subject	English
me gusta	*me gustan*	I like
te gusta	*te gustan*	you like
le gusta	*le gustan*	he, she, it likes; you like
nos gusta	*nos gustan*	we like
os gusta	*os gustan*	you like
les gusta	*les gustan*	they like; you like

The verb *gustar* isn't the only one to be used in this manner. Other verbs that commonly appear in this fashion are presented in the following table. The example given is in the present indicative, third-person singular subject, with *me* as the indirect object:

infinitive	example	translation
convenir	*me conviene*	it suits me
encantar	*me encanta*	I love it
faltar	*me falta*	I lack it
fascinar	*me fascina*	it fascinates me
importar	*me importa*	it's important to me

interesar	*me interesa*	it interests me
quedar	*me queda*	I have (it) left
tocar	*me toca*	it's my turn

Reflexive Verbs

If the verb's direct object refers to the same person as the subject, the verb is said to be reflexive—you might say that the object *reflects* back to the subject. You can recognize a reflexive verb by the reflexive pronoun that comes with it. In the infinitive, reflexive verbs end in *-se*. For example, *limpiar* means "to clean (something)," but *limpiarse* is translated as "to clean (yourself)." When a reflexive verb is conjugated, it is joined by the reflexive pronoun, which serves as the verb's object and follows the same rules as far as placement.

Reflexive Pronouns	
singular	**plural**
me (myself)	*nos* (ourselves)
te (yourself, informal)	*os* (yourselves, informal)
se (yourself, formal)	*se* (yourselves)
se (himself, herself, itself)	*se* (themselves)

 **ESSENTIAL**

Choosing the correct reflexive pronoun is easy—it should match the subject and the verb's conjugation in person and number: *él se afeita* (he shaves himself), *nosotros nos lavamos* (we wash ourselves).

Reflexives aren't common in English. You could say "I know myself," but there's no need to say "I dress myself"—we generally use "I get dressed" instead. In Spanish, reflexives are much more common.

Reflexive Verbs	
aburrirse	to be bored
acordarse	to remember
acostarse	to go to bed
afeitarse	to shave
alegrarse	to be happy
bañarse	to take a bath
cepillarse (los dientes, el cabello)	to brush (teeth, hair)
enojarse	to get angry
enterarse	to find out
fiarse de	to trust
lavarse	to wash
maquillarse	to put on makeup
molestarse	to get annoyed
mudarse	to move (change residence)
negarse a	to refuse
parecerse	to resemble
ponerse	to put on
quebrarse	to break (a bone)
quedarse	to remain
quemarse	to burn (oneself)
quitarse	to take off
romperse (la ropa)	to tear (clothes)
vestirse	to get dressed

Me ducho por las noches.

I take showers at night.

¿Usted se sorprende por las noticias?

Are you surprised by the news?

Some verbs are always used reflexively, but many more are reflexive only some of the time. In some cases, their meaning changes significantly. Here are some examples:

acercar (to move something closer)	*acercarse* (to approach)
arreglar (to arrange)	*arreglarse* (to get ready)
colocar (to put)	*colocarse* (to get a job, to find one's place)
despedir (to fire)	*despedirse* (to say goodbye)
detener (to bring to a halt)	*deternerse* (to come to a halt)
dormir (to sleep)	*dormirse* (to go to sleep)
lastimar (to hurt)	*lastimarse* (to bother oneself)
levantar (to raise, pick up)	*levantarse* (to get up)
reunir (to join, gather)	*reunirse* (to get together)

It's Reciprocal

Reflexive constructions are also used to indicate reciprocity. In English, this is done with the phrase "each other." A good example is the verb *casarse* (to get married):

Nos casamos hoy.

We are getting married today. (We are marrying each other today.)

In this case, *nos* is used reciprocally, rather than reflexively. Otherwise the sentence would mean "We are marrying ourselves today."

FACT

Reflexive verbs are most often used to talk about what is done to one's body, about one's emotions, and actions of motion: getting dressed (*vestirse*), to get angry (*enfadarse*), to jump (*tirarse*).

Make It Impersonal

Third-person reflexive pronoun *se* may be used in an impersonal construction *se* + verb. This is another alternative to using the passive voice, when you prefer not to specify who performs the action of the verb. Here is how you can change a sentence to make it impersonal:

La gente en Brasil habla portugués.
People in Brazil speak Portuguese.

En Brasil se habla portugués.
Portuguese is spoken in Brazil.

In the second sentence, *se* refers to Brazilians and *habla* is conjugated in third-person singular to agree with *portugués.* This constructions allows us to avoid having to refer specifically to Brazilian people as the subject of the verb *hablar*.

Here are other examples of this construction:

Se buscan empleados.

Employees are being looked for.

Se ven los problemas.

The problems are obvious.

Impersonal *se* constructions are often used in public signs: *No se fuma.* (No smoking.)

Practice Makes Perfect

Fill in the direct object pronoun:

1. *No tengo dinero. ________________ dejé en casa.*
2. *________________ dijeron (a mí) que llegará más tarde.*
3. *El taxista ________________ llevará (a ti) a casa.*
4. *Aquí tienes la revista. ________________ puedes leer más tarde.*
5. *Tengo muchas novelas. ________________ prefiero a la literatura no novelesca.*

Fill in the direct and indirect object pronoun:

1. *La enfermera trae las pastillas a nosotros.*

   ________________ trae.
2. *Ellos necesitan ayuda.*

   ¿ ________________ das?
3. *Quieres conducir el coche.*

   Yo ____________ presto.
4. *Ellos dicen la verdad a vosotros.*

   Ellos ________________ dicen.

5. *Explico el cuento a Marta y Pedro.*

   ____________ *explico.*

Translate into Spanish:

1. I like to dance.

   ____

2. She loves flowers.

   ____

3. You (informal) have five dollars left.

   ____

4. They lack money.

   ____

5. We are interested in your stories.

   ____

Fill in the correct reflexive verb and reflexive pronoun:

1. *Ustedes* ____________ *(cepillarse) los dientes dos veces por día.*
2. *Nosotros* ____________ *(mudarse) a Nueva York el próximo junio.*
3. *Ramón* ____________ *(afeitarse) cada mañana.*
4. *Ellos* ____________ *(enterarse) de todos mis secretos.*
5. *Nuestro jefe* ____________ *(vestirse) bien, aún los fines de semana.*

To check your answers, refer to the answer key in Appendix D.

Chapter 11
In the Past

AT THIS POINT, you've reviewed many types of verb and verbal constructions in the context of the present tense. The next few chapters will review other tenses—the past, future, conditional, and compound tenses—as well as subjunctive and command moods.

Let's begin with the past tense. In Spanish, there are a few ways to express actions occurring in past tense. In addition to the compound past tenses (covered in Chapter 14), Spanish past tenses include preterite, imperfect, and past progressives.

What You Did—the Preterite

The preterite tense, *el pretérito*, is used to describe actions that occurred and were completed in the past:

Ernesto llegó al restaurante a las cinco.

Ernesto arrived at the restaurant at five.

Ya acabó la película.

The movie ended already.

Conocí a Eliana en una de las fiestas de Javier.

I met Eliana at one of Javier's parties.

For each of these sentences, the action is definite and refers to an event that happened at a particular time, not one that took place regularly. To distinguish preterite tense from other past tenses in Spanish, you might want to think of it as the concrete past, used to describe particular events and actions. (More on the differences between the preterite and the imperfect past is to follow later in the chapter.)

Preterite Endings

To conjugate verbs in the preterite, drop the infinitive ending and add the appropriate preterite ending. Note that –ER and –IR verbs share identical endings:

–AR Verbs		–ER and –IR Verbs	
é	amos	í	imos
aste	asteis	iste	isteis
ó	aron	ió	ieron

Irregular Forms

The preterite conjugations have quite a few irregularities, but not as many as the present indicative forms. For instance, –AR and –ER verbs do not undergo a vowel change (e > ie or o > ue) in the stem.

Vowel Change in –IR Verbs

Remember verbs like *gemir* (to moan), *repetir* (to repeat), *mentir* (to lie), and *preferir* (to prefer)? The first two undergo a e > i change, while the last pair are e > ie verbs. All of these verbs have an e > i irregularity in the preterite, but the trick is this: Only the third-person forms undergo the vowel change:

gemí	*gemimos*
gemiste	*gemisteis*
gimió	*gimieron*

preferí	*preferimos*
preferiste	*preferisteis*
prefirió	*prefirieron*

The same kind of change occurs with –IR verbs that have an o > u stem change in the present indicative. Again, the change only affects third-person conjugations in the preterite. Take a look at preterite conjugations of *dormir* (to sleep) and *morir* (to die):

dormí	*dormimos*
dormiste	*dormisteis*
durmió	*durmieron*

morí	*morimos*
moriste	*moristeis*
murió	*murieron*

Spelling Modification Verbs

All but one preterite ending begins with "i"; the only exception is –é (first person singular of –AR verbs). This is why –AR verbs with a stem that ends in c, g, or z require a spelling modification conjugated in the *yo* form to retain correct pronunciation with the –é ending.

In –AR verbs with a stem ending in "c" like *explicar* (to explain) and *tocar* (to touch), the final consonant changes to "qu":

expliqué	*explicamos*
explicaste	*explicasteis*
explicó	*explicaron*

toqué	*tocamos*
tocaste	*tocasteis*
tocó	*tocaron*

If the –AR verb's stem ends with a "g," a "u" is added to the ending of the *yo* form. Again, this is done to retain the hard "g" pronunciation. Take a look at the conjugations of the verbs *jugar* (to play) and *pagar* (to pay):

jugué	*jugamos*
jugaste	*jugasteis*
jugó	*jugaron*

pagué	*pagamos*
pagaste	*pagasteis*
pagó	*pagaron*

The third group of –AR verbs that undergo a similar spelling change in the *yo* form includes verbs with a stem ending in "z." In this case, the stem ending changes to "c." Examples here are *cruzar* (to cross) and *realizar* (to realize):

crucé	*cruzamos*
cruzaste	*cruzasteis*
cruzó	*cruzaron*

realicé	*realizamos*
realizaste	*realizasteis*
realizó	*realizaron*

Spelling modification also occurs in –ER and –IR verbs that have a stem ending in a vowel, such as the –uir verbs. The spelling change is in the ending: In the third-person forms, the "i" of the ending changes to a "y." For example, here are the conjugations of *concluir* (to conclude) and *huir* (to flee):

concluí	*concluimos*
concluiste	*concluisteis*
concluyó	*concluyeron*

huí	*huimos*
huiste	*huisteis*
huyó	*huyeron*

QUESTION?

Is there a preterite form of *hay* (there is, there are)?
Yes, the preterite form is *hubo.* For example: *Hubo de todo: violencia, amor, tristeza.* (There was a little bit of everything—violence, love, sadness.) Note that the sentence refers to a specific event. The imperfect form of this verb is more frequently used.

Other verbs with a stem ending in a vowel include *leer* (to read) and *oír* (to hear). They follow the same change, plus require extra accent marks to retain the stress over the "i":

leí	*leímos*
leíste	*leísteis*
leyó	*leyeron*

oí	*oímos*
oíste	*oísteis*
oyó	*oyeron*

A Group of Their Own

A set of verbs—including –AR, –ER, and –IR verbs—have irregular conjugations in the preterite, including an irregular stem and a slightly different set of endings. These endings are:

–e	–imos
–iste	–isteis
–o	–ieron

These endings are very similar to the regular preterite –ER and –IR verb endings, except for the *yo* form and the lack of accent marks in some of the forms. The endings are added to a modified stem:

infinitive	preterite stem	translation
andar	*anduv–*	to walk
caber	*cup–*	to fit
decir	*dij–*	to say
estar	*estuv–*	to be
hacer	*hic– (hiz–)*	to do
poder	*pud–*	to be able to
poner	*pus–*	to put
producir	*produj–*	to produce
querer	*quis–*	to want
saber	*sup–*	to know
tener	*tuv–*	to have
traer	*traj–*	to bring
venir	*vin–*	to arrive

 **ESSENTIAL**

The irregular verbs listed here may also follow additional irregularities based on spelling modification rules discussed earlier. For example, *hacer* (to do) becomes *hizo* in the third-person singular (*él, ella, Ud.*) conjugation.

pude	*pudimos*
pudiste	*pudisteis*
pudo	*pudieron*

produje	*produjimos*
produjiste	*produjisteis*
produjo	*produjeron*

Note that other verbs ending in –ucir will also follow the same irregularity as the *producir* in the third-person plural form. The "i" drops out from the ending to retain the hard "h" sound of the Spanish letter "j."

Completely Irregular

In addition to the verbs covered so far, a few more have their own irregularities. *Dar* (to give) takes on –ER/–IR verb endings, but without the accent marks; *ver* (to see) also drops the accent marks. Finally, *ser* (to be) and *ir* (to go) share the same forms in the preterite tense, and the stem looks nothing like either of the verbs–it's "fu–."

di	*dimos*
diste	*disteis*
dio	*dieron*

vi	*vimos*
viste	*visteis*
vio	*vieron*

fui	*fuimos*
fuiste	*fuisteis*
fue	*fueron*

What You Were Doing—the Imperfect

The alternative to the preterite tense is the imperfect. This version of the Spanish past tense is used to describe ongoing past actions, or actions that occurred habitually. Here are a few examples of the imperfect tense in action:

Estudiábamos juntos casi todos los días.
Almost every day we studied together.

En los años setenta, ellos vivían en la calle Main.
In the seventies, they lived on Main Street.

Mientras ella miraba la televisión, yo terminaba mis tareas.
While she was watching television, I was finishing my chores.

Conjugating verbs in the imperfect tense is very easy. All you need to do is drop the infinitive ending and add the proper imperfect ending:

–AR Verbs		–ER and –IR Verbs	
–aba	–ábamos	–ía	–íamos
–abas	–abais	–ías	–íais
–aba	–aban	–ía	–ían

The only irregularly conjugated verbs are *ir* (to go), *ser* (to be), and *ver* (to see):

iba	*íbamos*
ibas	*ibais*
iba	*iban*

era	*éramos*
eras	*erais*
era	*eran*

veía	*veíamos*
veías	*veíais*
veía	*veían*

Also, as you might have noticed from one of the example sentences, the imperfect form of *hay* is *había.*

FACT

You can use the imperfect tense to talk about the time or date when a certain event took place. For example: *¿Qué hora era cuando te enteraste qué pasó?* (What time was it when you found out what happened?)

A Point of Comparison

The easiest way to understand the differences between preterite and imperfect tenses is to see them used together in the same sentence:

Estaba en la cama cuando oí los ruidos.

I was in bed when I heard the sounds.

Teresa anunció ayer que pensaba recomenzar sus estudios.

Yesterday Teresa announced that she was thinking of returning to her studies.

Generalmente, llegaba al trabajo a tiempo, pero aquel día llegué muy tarde.

Generally, I arrived to work on time, but that day I arrived very late.

In the first example, the imperfect is used to show the continual action (I was in bed) while the preterite illustrates the specific action (I heard the sounds). In the second example, the imperfect is used to describe Teresa's general thoughts over a period of time, while the preterite describes the specific action of making the announcement. In the third example, the imperfect form of *llegar* shows habitual action, while the same verb in the preterite tense describes a specific action on one particular day.

It's Not the Same Thing

A few of the verbs change in meaning depending on whether they are in the preterite or the imperfect form. Compare the following pair:

Conoció a Jorge en Toledo.

She met Jorge in Toledo.

Conocía a Jorge por mucho tiempo.

She knew Jorge for a very long time.

In the preterite, which signals a specific action, *conocer* is translated as "to meet." In the imperfect, the past tense of ongoing actions, *conocer* indicates how long you've known someone or something. The same changes of meaning can be seen in *poder* (to be able to), *saber* (to know), and *tener* (to have):

No pude completar los ejercicios.

I didn't manage to complete the exercises.

No podía completar los ejercicios.

I wasn't able to complete the exercises.

Supe la verdad demasiado tarde.

I found out the truth too late.

No sabía la verdad.

I didn't know the truth.

Tuvimos una idea.

We got an idea.

Teníamos mucha hambre.

We were very hungry.

Past Progressive Forms

Just as there are two past-tense forms of *hay* (there is, there are), there are also two versions of the progressive form: the preterite progressive and the imperfect progressive. As you might recall from Chapter 9, progressive forms of the verb are formed with the verb *estar* (to be), plus the present participle.

Of the two forms, by far the more common one is the imperfect progressive. This makes sense, because the imperfect tense is used to describe ongoing actions:

Estaba cocinando la cena.

She was cooking dinner.

Estaba trabajando cuando oí las noticias.

I was working when I heard the news.

The preterite progressive is less common, but it also has its uses. You can use it to show action that was in progress in the past but was then completed:

Estuve trabajando hasta que oí las noticias.

I was working until I heard the news.

Practice Makes Perfect

Conjugate the verbs in parentheses; choose between the preterite and imperfect tense:

1. *¿(Tú) ________________ (dormir) un rato?*
2. *Hace tres años que nuestra abuela ______________ (morirse).*
3. *La maestra nunca ____________________ (cansarse) de nuestras preguntas.*
4. *Generalmente la enfermera _________________ (comer) el desayuno a las ocho.*
5. *Yo____________________ (pensar) terminar el trabajo a las cinco, pero____________ (terminar) a las siete.*
6. *Cuando______________ (estar) en el grupo de rock, yo ______________ (tocar) la guitarra y Ernesto ______________ (tocar) la batería.*
7. *¿Ya (ella) te __________________ (decir) qué pasó?*
8. *¿Ustedes ____________________ (leer) la novela Rayuela de Julio Cortázar?*
9. *Los clases ____________________ (acabar) en junio.*
10. *Nosotros _____________________ (dar) el dinero a la camarera.*
11. *En aquellos días, ellos _______________ (preferir) el cine a los libros.*
12. *Usted _______________ (estar) trabajando cuando se ______________ (apagarse) la luz.*
13. *Los niños______________ (estar) en cama cuando ______________ (oír) los ruidos.*
14. *Yo____________________ (conocer) a mi marido en la fiesta de Navidad.*

15. *El año pasado, yo ___________(dormir) por lo menos ocho horas cada noche.*
16. *Ellos _______________(venir) por la noche.*
17. *_______________ (haber) mucha comida para los invitados.*
18. *El gerente ___________(concluir) su lectura con aplausos.*
19. *Yo siempre ___________(decir) que no tendrás suerte en este proyecto.*
20. *Mientras nosotros ___________(caminar) a casa, _______________(empezar) a llover.*

To check your answers, refer to the answer key in Appendix D.

CHAPTER 12

Future and Conditional

THE NEXT TWO TENSES to review are simple future tense and conditional tense. Both have equivalents in English and both are easy to conjugate—only a few Spanish verbs are irregular in the future and conditional tense, and in each case, the irregularity remains the same in both of these tenses.

Double Endings

Because conjugating verbs in the future and conditional is very similar, it makes sense to introduce them together. In both sets of conjugations, the verb retains its infinitive ending and takes on an additional ending according to its person and number. What makes things really simple is that –AR, –ER, and –IR verbs share the same set of endings:

Future Tense Endings		Conditional Tense Endings	
–é	–emos	–ía	–íamos
–ás	–éis	–ías	–íais
–á	–án	–ía	–ían

In English, these tenses are formed with compound verbs. To form the future tense, you use "will + verb"; to form the conditional, you use "would + verb." In Spanish, these tenses don't require compound forms. All you need to know are the endings.

Irregular Stem Forms

There is another reason conjugating verbs in the future and the conditional is relatively easy—the few verbs that are irregular vary from the infinitive form, but retain the same regular endings. Furthermore, the same infinitive form change applies to conjugations in both tenses.

infinitive	future/conditional stem	English
caber	*cabr–*	to fit
decir	*dir–*	to say
hacer	*har–*	to do
haber	*habr–*	to have (compound tense verb)
poder	*podr–*	to be able to
poner	*pondr–*	to put
querer	*querr–*	to want
saber	*sabr–*	to know
salir	*saldr–*	to go out
tener	*tendr–*	to have
valer	*valdr–*	to be worth
venir	*vendr–*	to come

QUESTION?

Why do these verbs have irregular stems?

In most irregular verbs, the resulting stem is shorter than the infinitive, making it easier to pronounce. For example, instead of *poneré,* the conjugation is shortened to *pondré* (I will put); instead of *decirás,* the correct form is *dirás* (you would say).

Future Actions in the Present

Now that we've got the conjugation basics down, let's move on to the verb tenses. First up is the future tense. But you don't necessarily need to use the grammatical future tense (simple future) to express actions that will take place in the future. Let's review your options.

Present Tense

As you've learned in Chapter 7, you can actually use the present tense to talk about actions that will happen in the immediate future. You might not have noticed, but we do the same in English:

Regresamos a la escuela el lunes.

We go back to school on Monday.

Plans for the Future

The expression "going to" isn't exactly future tense, but it does deal with actions one plans to do in the future. In Spanish, an equivalent expression is *ir a* + infinitive:

Voy a decirle lo que pienso.

I will tell her what I think. (I am going to tell her what I think.)

Simple Future

The simple future tense, *el futuro,* is used to express actions that will take place in the future. To review the future tense conjugations, here are the conjugations of regular verbs *hablar* (to speak), *vender* (to sell), and *vivir* (to live), as well as an irregular ver, *decir* (to say). A few examples of the future tense in action follow.

hablaré	*hablaremos*
hablarás	*hablaréis*
hablará	*hablarán*

venderé	*venderemos*
venderás	*venderéis*
venderá	*venderán*

viviré	*viviremos*
vivirás	*viviréis*
vivirá	*vivirán*

diré	*diremos*
dirás	*diréis*
dirá	*dirán*

¿Cuándo acabarás con los ejercicios?

When will you be done with the exercises?

Tendremos que terminar todo antes de cenar.

We will have to finish everything before dinnertime.

It's Anyone's Guess

Paradoxically, the simple future tense may be used to for guessing or conjecture about actions in the present tense. Compare the following:

¿Dónde está tu hermana? Está en casa. Estará en casa.

Where is your sister? She is home. She's probably home.

The second of the two answers doesn't mean "she will be home"; in this case, the future tense makes the statement less certain.

ESSENTIAL

You'll be able to tell whether a verb conjugated in the future tense refers to an uncertain present action or to an action in the future as long as you pay attention to the context.

It's Potential

The conditional tense, *el potencial simple,* is conjugated the same as the future tense, except for the different endings. Take a look at our four sample verbs, *hablar* (to speak), *vender* (to sell), *vivir* (to live), and *decir* (to say):

hablaría	*hablaríamos*
hablarías	*hablaríais*
hablaría	*hablarían*

vendería	*venderíamos*
venderías	*venderíais*
vendería	*venderían*

viviría	*viviríamos*
vivirías	*viviríais*
viviría	*vivirían*

diría	*diríamos*
dirías	*diríais*
diría	*dirían*

The conditional is used to express the Spanish equivalent of "would + verb" (except in the sense of something that "used to be" done). It's a tense of potentialities, of something that would happen on the condition of something else taking place:

¿Qué harían?

What would you do?

Quisiera un helado.

I would like an ice cream.

Conditional tense is also used to express guessing or conjecture, except that it takes place in the past. Compare the following:

¿Dónde estuvo tu hermana? Estuvo en casa. Estaría en casa.

Where was your sister? She was at home. She was probably at home.

QUESTION?

What is a subordinate clause?
A clause is a part of a sentence, often separated from other parts by a conjunction like "and" or "or," or by punctuation like a semicolon. Whereas a main clause can stand on its own as a complete sentence, a subordinate clause depends on the main clause for meaning. In if/then sentences, the "if" clause is the subordinate clause.

Future and Conditional Clauses

Conditional tense is often used in sentences with subordinate clauses. (To a lesser degree, this is also true of future tense.) Subordinate clauses in the conditional are always paired off with the past-tense main clause. Future-tense subordinate clauses go with a present-tense main clause. Here is one common example:

Yo sabía lo que harían.

I knew what they would do.

Yo sé lo que harán.

I know what they will do.

If, Then

Future and conditional are also used in "if . . . then" clauses. When the "if" clause is in the present tense, the "then" clause has a future-tense verb:

Si consigo trabajo, compraré un coche nuevo.

If I get a job, I will buy a new car.

The conditional version of this is a little trickier–you'll need to use the imperfect subjunctive (presented in Appendix A) in the "if" clause:

Si fuera rico, compraría un coche nuevo.

If I were rich, I would buy a new car.

Practice Makes Perfect

Conjugate the following verbs (in parentheses) in the future tense:

1. *El armario no ________________ (caber) aquí.*
2. *Nosotros ______________________ (saber) lo que pasó cuando encontremos a María.*
3. ______________________ *(haber) tiempo mañana.*
4. *Yo ____________________ (tener) la respuesta el próximo día.*
5. ______________________ *(ponerse) tu nuevo traje, ¿verdad?*

Conjugate the following verbs (in parentheses) in the conditional tense:

1. *Yo no lo* ______________ *(decir) si no fuera la verdad.*
2. *Si pudiera, ella* ______________ *(venir) hoy.*
3. *Esto no* ______________ *(valer) la pena.*
4. *¿Ustedes* ______________ *(querer) empezar la lectura ya?*
5. *Nosotros* ______________ *(hacer) todo si tuviéramos el tiempo.*

Translate the following sentences into English:

1. *Todos irán a la fiesta.*

____

2. *Yo vendré al restaurante a las siete.*

____

3. *Yo lo haría contigo.*

____

4. *Nosotros visitaríamos a nuestros abuelos el jueves.*

____

To check your answers, refer to the answer key in Appendix D.

CHAPTER 13

In the Mood—Subjunctive and Imperative

SO FAR, YOU'VE BEEN REVIEWING verb tenses in the indicative mood–the mood that indicates what is, was, or will be. But there are two other grammatical moods in English as well as in Spanish: subjunctive and imperative. Subjunctive mood is reserved for making statements where the action is potential or uncertain. Imperative mood is the mood of command.

The Subjunctive Mood

A lot of people who speak English as their native language don't realize that English grammar includes the subjunctive mood, so when they start learning Spanish, they have a difficult time understanding what this mood is for and how it should be used. But we do occasionally use the subjunctive–it's just that in English, subjunctive mood is on the decline and rarely used.

Take a look at the following example:

If Janet were sorry, she would have said so.

The correct past tense conjugation of "to be" in third person singular should be "was," and yet the verb used here is "were." Why? The statement "Janet was sorry" isn't technically correct–the speaker does not actually know whether Janet was in fact sorry. This is why the statement is presented in the subjunctive mood–to show grammatically that it isn't certain. Here's another example:

Janet's parents demand that she clean her room.

Again, why isn't the verb here "cleans"? The reason is that the verb is actually in the subjunctive mood. Janet's parents demand that she do something, but it's uncertain whether she'll actually do it.

As you can see, the subjunctive mood may come in present tense ("she clean") or in past tense ("she were"). This is also true in Spanish.

FACT

Subjunctive mood is also retained in a few commonly used phrases, like "if I were you," "God help us," and "come what may." In all of these cases, the statements refer to a potential reality that may or may not occur, and you can see that they're in the subjunctive mood because the verbs are "were" and not "was," "help" and not "helps," and "come"—not "comes."

Because English verbs aren't heavily inflected (they don't have very many conjugated forms and endings), the subjunctive mood is almost invisible. In fact, some grammarians argue that in our language it's on the way out. Often, a subjunctive mood may be expressed with verbs like "may" or "should" instead of changing the conjugation of the active verb:

She should clean her room.

What may come will come.

The resistance to the subjunctive doesn't occur in Spanish, however—this mood continues to thrive among speakers of Spanish, and you'll encounter it quite often.

Present Subjunctive

The present subjunctive in Spanish is known as *el presente de subjuntivo*. The conjugations in this tense are similar to the present indicative tense, but with a few interesting differences. The most important of these differences is that the endings are inverted. This means -AR verbs have endings beginning with "e" and -ER and -IR verbs have endings that start with "a." Another difference is that the *yo* and *él/ella/usted* forms are identical.

–AR Verbs		–ER and –IR Verbs	
–e	–emos	–a	–amos
–es	–éis	–as	–áis
–e	–en	–a	–an

To illustrate the conjugations, here are *hablar* (to speak), *vender* (to sell), and *vivir* (to live), conjugated in the present subjunctive:

Hablar	
hable	*hablemos*
hables	*habléis*
hable	*hablen*

Vender	
venda	*vendamos*
vendas	*vendáis*
venda	*vendan*

Vivir	
viva	*vivamos*
vivas	*viváis*
viva	*vivan*

Use the Right Stem

The stem used in the subjunctive is generally identical to the *yo* form of the present indicative. This means that verbs irregular in the *yo* form of the present indicative retain the same stem irregularity in all forms of the present subjunctive.

Infinitive	Present Indicative (yo form)	Present Subjunctive (yo form)
Verbs that end in –uir (i > y)		
atribuir (to attribute)	*atribuyo*	*atribuya*
concluir (to conclude)	*concluyo*	*concluya*
huir (to flee)	*huyo*	*huya*
influir (to influence)	*influyo*	*influya*
sustituir (to substitute)	*sustituyo*	*sustituya*
Verbs that end in –ecer or –ucir (c > zc)		
aparecer (to appear)	*aparezco*	*aparezca*
conducir (to drive)	*conduzco*	*conduzca*
conocer (to know)	*conozco*	*conozca*
crecer (to grow)	*crezco*	*crezca*
establecer (to establish)	*establezco*	*establezca*
parecer (to seem)	*parezco*	*parezca*
traducir (to translate)	*traduzco*	*traduzca*
Verbs that end in –ger or –gir (g > j)		
coger (to grab)	*cojo*	*coja*
dirigir (to direct)	*dirijo*	*dirija*
fingir (to pretend)	*finjo*	*finja*
proteger (to protect)	*protejo*	*proteja*

Verbs that end in –iar or –uar		
actuar (to act)	*actúo*	*actúe*
confiar (to confide)	*confío*	*confíe*
continuar (to continue)	*continúo*	*continúe*
espiar (to spy)	*espío*	*espíe*
enviar (to send)	*envío*	*envíe*
Verbs that gain a "g" in the stem (–ER and –IR verbs)		
caer (to fall)	*caigo*	*caiga*
decir (to say)	*digo*	*diga*
hacer (to do)	*hago*	*haga*
oír (to hear)	*oigo*	*oiga*
poner (to put)	*pongo*	*ponga*
salir (to leave)	*salgo*	*salga*
tener (to have)	*tengo*	*tenga*
traer (to bring)	*traigo*	*traiga*
valer (to cost)	*valgo*	*valga*
venir (to come)	*vengo*	*venga*
Stem-changing –IR verbs (e > i)		
gemir (to moan)	*gimo*	*gima*
pedir (to ask)	*pido*	*pida*
repetir (to repeat)	*repito*	*repita*
vestir (to dress)	*visto*	*vista*
Other verbs irregular in the *yo* form of present indicative		
caber (to fit)	*quepo*	*quepa*
reír (to laugh)	*río*	*ría*
ver (to see)	*veo*	*vea*

When conjugating any of these verbs—plus other verbs belonging to the same irregular-verb group—keep in mind that the stem remains the same in all six conjugations and the subjunctive endings are regular. Take two examples, the verb *establecer* (to establish) and *ver* (to see):

establezca	*establezcamos*
establezcas	*establezcáis*
establezca	*establezcan*

vea	*veamos*
veas	*veáis*
vea	*vean*

However, not all verbs follow this rule. There are others that behave even more unpredictably.

ESSENTIAL

It's easy to get confused with the indicative and subjunctive forms of the present tense. When you're in doubt, always think back to the infinitive form. If you've got an –AR verb, "a" endings are indicative and "e" endings are subjunctive. If you've got an –ER or –IR verb, the opposite is true.

Irregular Present-Subjunctive Forms

There are three additional groups of irregular verbs in the present subjunctive. Some verbs also use the *yo* form of the present indicative as its model, but do so in four out of six conjugations–*nosotros* and *vosotros* forms either remain regular or undergo a different stem change.

The second group undergoes a spelling change in accordance with the spelling modification rules (covered in the review of irregular verbs in the present tense). The third group does not share its stem with the *yo* form of the present indicative–stems of the verbs in this group are unique to the present subjunctive conjugations and must be memorized.

Stem-Change Irregularities

Some –AR and –ER verbs that undergo a stem change (e > ie, o >ue) in the *yo* form of the present indicative do have the same change in the present subjunctive, but they do not exhibit the stem change in *nosotros* and *vosotros* forms.

Let's begin with the verbs with an e > ie stem change. Take a look at the conjugations of *apretar* (to grip) and *defender* (to defend):

apriete	*apretemos*
aprietes	*apretéis*
apriete	*aprieten*

defienda	*defendamos*
defiendas	*defendáis*
defienda	*defiendan*

Other e > ie stem-changing verbs that behave the same way in the present subjunctive include the following:

Infinitive	Present Indicative (*yo* form)	Present Subjunctive (*yo* form)	Present Subjunctive (*nosotros* form)
atravesar (to cross)	*atravieso*	*atraviese*	*atravesemos*
cerrar (to close)	*cierro*	*cierre*	*cerremos*
encender (to light)	*enciendo*	*encienda*	*encendamos*
gobernar (to govern)	*gobierno*	*gobierne*	*gobernemos*
pensar (to think)	*pienso*	*piense*	*pensemos*
perder (to lose)	*pierdo*	*pierda*	*perdamos*
querer (to want)	*quiero*	*quiera*	*queramos*
sentar (to sit)	*siento*	*siente*	*sentemos*

–AR and –ER verbs with the o > ue stem change follow the same "four out of six" rule. Take a look at the present-subjunctive conjugations of *contar* (to count, to tell) and *poder* (to be able to):

cuente	*contemos*
cuentes	*contéis*
cuente	*cuenten*

pueda	*podamos*
puedas	*podáis*
pueda	*puedan*

Other verbs that behave in the same fashion include the following:

Infinitive	Present Indicative (*yo* form)	Present Subjunctive (*yo* form)	Present Subjunctive (*nosotros* form)
costar (to cost)	*cuesto*	*cueste*	*costemos*
doler (to hurt)	*duelo*	*duela*	*dolamos*
mostrar (to show)	*muestro*	*muestre*	*mostremos*
recordar (to remember)	*recuerdo*	*recuerda*	*recordemos*
volar (to fly)	*vuelo*	*vuele*	*volemos*
volver (to return)	*vuelvo*	*vuelva*	*volvamos*

The rule for stem-changing –IR verbs is a little different. In the *nosotros* and *vosotros* forms, the stem vowel changes as follows: e > i, o > u. Here are two examples, *mentir* (to lie) and *dormir* (to sleep):

mienta	*mintamos*
mientas	*mintáis*
mienta	*mientan*

duerma	*durmamos*
duermas	*durmáis*
duerma	*duerman*

Infinitive	Present Indicative (*yo* form)	Present Subjunctive (*yo* form)	Present Subjunctive (*nosotros* form)
morir (to die)	*muero*	*muera*	*muramos*
preferir (to prefer)	*prefiero*	*prefiera*	*prefiramos*
sentir (to feel)	*siento*	*sienta*	*sintamos*

Spelling-Modification Irregularities

For some verbs, there's a spelling modification that does not occur with the *yo* form of the present indicative, but which does occur in other forms and which is necessary in the present subjunctive. The letters involved in the spelling modification are "c," "g," and "z," and they are found at the end of the stem, where their interaction with the endings results in the change.

When you're conjugating an –AR verb in the present subjunctive, the "e" in the endings requires the following changes:

c > qu

g > gu

z > c

For example, take a look at the conjugations of *tocar* (to touch), *llegar* (to arrive), and *cruzar* (to cross):

toque	*toquemos*
toques	*toquéis*
toque	*toquen*

llegue	*lleguemos*
llegues	*lleguéis*
llegue	*lleguen*

cruce	*crucemos*
cruces	*crucéis*
cruce	*crucen*

Alternatively, –ER and –IR verbs might require one of the following changes, brought on by the endings that begin with "a":

c > z

g > j

gu > g

To illustrate how this works, here are the conjugations of *conocer* (to know), *proteger* (to protect), and *seguir* (to follow):

conozca	conozcamos
conozcas	conozcáis
conozca	conozcan

proteja	*protejamos*
protejas	*protejáis*
proteja	*protejan*

siga	*sigamos*
sigas	*sigáis*
siga	*sigan*

 **FACT**

Some verbs have both a stem change and a spelling modification change. Take the verb *empezar* (to begin): its six conjugations in the subjunctive are *empiece, empieces, empiece, empecemos, empecéis,* and *empiecen.*

Other Irregularities

A small group of verbs have an irregular stem that you'll need to memorize; these verbs retain the regular present-subjunctive endings.

Infinitive	present-subjunctive stem	*yo* form
haber (to have)	*hay–*	*haya*
ir (to go)	*vay–*	*vaya*
saber (to know)	*sep–*	*sepa*
ser (to be)	*se–*	*sea*

Three other verbs—*dar* (to give), *estar* (to be), and *oler* (to smell)—have irregular present subjunctive forms. Their conjugations are:

dé	*demos*
des	*deis*
dé	*den*

esté	*estemos*
estés	*estéis*
esté	*estén*

huela	*olamos*
huelas	*oláis*
huela	*huelan*

Indicative or Subjunctive?

The rule of thumb when choosing between indicative and subjunctive is to ask yourself whether the verb is used to describe a state or action that is concrete (whether it takes place in the past, present, or future doesn't make any difference here) or whether it is potential and/or subjective. For example, compare the two statements:

Yo sé que Alana está bien.

I know that Alana is well.

Yo espero que Alana esté bien.

I hope that Alana is well.

In the first example, the statement refers to something that is known—that Alana is well. The second statement isn't describing something that's definite. It is merely expressing hope that Alana is well—whether she is in fact well isn't the point here. In Spanish, this kind of uncertainty requires the use of the subjunctive.

Sometimes the only difference between the indicative and subjunctive is a simple "no." *Es cierto que* (it's certain that) should be followed by a phrase in the indicative mood; *no es cierto que* (it's not certain that) is a phrase that introduces a clause in the subjunctive mood.

Two Verbs Connected with *Que*

Present subjunctive is frequently used within a *que* (that) clause, as in the previous example. Whether or not the *que* clause should have a subjunctive-mood verb depends on the verb in the main clause. Here's another example:

Ella duda que tú entiendas la lección.

She doubts you understand the lesson.

Because the sentence's main action is *dudar* (to doubt), the verb *entender* (to understand) inside the *que* clause is in the subjunctive mood. Several different groups of verbs generally take on a subjunctive *que* clause:

Doubt or Uncertainty	
dudar	to doubt
no estar seguro	not to be sure
imaginarse	to expect

Hope or Necessity	
esperar	to hope, to expect
necesitar	to need
querer	to want
preferir	to prefer

Emotional State	
alegrar	to make happy
enojar	to make angry
gustar	to like
sentir	to feel
sorprender	to surprise

Telling or Asking	
aconsejar	to advise
decir	to say
exigir	to demand
insistir	to insist
pedir	to ask
prohibir	to forbid
rogar	to beg

ESSENTIAL

If the subject of the main verb and the dependent verb match, the *que* clause is dropped and the dependent verb remains in the infinitive form. Compare: *Quiero que vayan a la obra de teatro.* (I want them to go to the theater performance.) *Quiero ir a la obra de teatro.* (I want to go to the theater performance.) In the second example, the subjunctive mood isn't necessary.

Here are a few examples to help you see how this works:

No estoy seguro que ellos tengan su propia tienda de campaña.
I'm not sure that they have their own tent.

Prefiero que haga sol.
I prefer it to be sunny.

Tú siempre quieres que tus hijos se comporten bien.
You always want your kids to behave well.

Mona nos pide que la ayudemos a coser los disfraces.

Mona asks us to help her sew the costumes.

Impersonal Constructions

When the main clause is an impersonal construction with no clear subject, the *que* clause may be in the subjunctive mood to show that the statement is hypothetical or potential, or to show the speaker's attitude or emotion. Common impersonal phrases that are frequently used with the subjunctive include the following:

es bueno que	it's good that
es dudoso que	it's doubtful that
es importante que	it's important that
es malo que	it's bad that
es mejor que	it's better that
es necesario que	it's necessary that
es probable que	it's probable that
es triste que	it's sad that
es una lástima que	it's a pity that

Here are two examples:

Es bueno que mi hermana no esté enferma.

It's good that my sister isn't ill.

Es necesario que ustedes se laven las manos antes de comer.

It's necessary for you to wash your hands before eating.

In impersonal constructions, the verb inside the *que* clause must have a subject (in the previous examples, the subjects are *mi hermana* and *ustedes*). If there's no subject–that is, if the second part of the sentence following *que* is also impersonal–the infinitive is used instead. Compare the following:

Es importante que ustedes lleguen a tiempo.

It's important that you arrive on time.

Es importante llegar a tiempo.

It's important to arrive on time.

FACT

Subjunctive mood is sometimes translated with the word "might." For example: *Ellos parecen cansados; tal vez tengan hambre.* (They look tired; they might be hungry.) Note that the first part of the sentence is in the indicative mood—the speaker indicates how "they" look. The second part, in the subjunctive, is less certain—it's just a guess the speaker is making.

Subjunctive Mood in Adverbial Clauses

An adverbial clause is a clause (or group of words) that modifies the verb. In some adverbial clauses that include a verb, the verb should be conjugated in the subjunctive mood. Take a look at the following example:

Marisa rega los flores para que no se marchiten.

Marisa waters the flowers so that they don't wilt.

As you can see, *no se marchiten* is introduced by the conjunction *para que* and not *que*. Other conjunctions that make the adverbial phrase subjunctive include these:

a fin de que	in order that
a menos que	unless
antes (de) que	before
con tal (de) que	provided that
como	as
cuando	when
en caso de que	in case
sin que	without

In addition, the following conjunctions may require the use of subjunctive in the adverbial clause, depending on context:

aunque	although
como	how
de manera que	so that
donde	where
mientras	while
según	according to

For example, compare the following two sentences. The first one has an indicative adverbial clause; the second one is in the subjunctive.

Aunque nieva, voy a llegar en coche.

Even though it is snowing, I'll come by car.

Aunque nieve, voy a llegar en coche.

Even if it may snow, I'll come by car.

 **ESSENTIAL**

Some *que* clauses are actually adjective clauses—clauses that modify a noun. For example, in the following example, the *que* clause modifies the noun *libro: Busco un libro que explique la gramática del castellano.* (I'm looking for a book that explains Spanish grammar.)

Past Subjunctive

The subjunctive mood may also be expressed in the past with the help of *el imperfecto de subjuntivo* (the imperfect or past subjunctive). Whereas the present subjunctive is used with present-tense indicative verbs in the main clause, the past subjunctive appears in *que* clauses introduced by a verb in the imperfect, preterite, past perfect, or conditional tense. First, let's look at how verbs in the past subjunctive are conjugated.

Two Groups of Conjugations

The past subjunctive is the only tense/mood where you've got two sets of endings to choose from. Both sets are equally correct; choosing one over the other will not change the meaning, although some say that the –ra endings tend to be more common in colloquial speech.

The good news, however, is that even though there are two sets of endings to choose from, each set may be used with –AR, –ER, and –IR verbs:

–ra	–ramos
–ras	–rais
–ra	–ran

–se	–semos
–ses	–seis
–se	–sen

To form the conjugation, take the third-person plural *(ellos)* form of the preterite, drop the –ron ending, and add the correct past-subjunctive ending. Let's take *hablar* as an example: The preterite *ellos* form is *hablaron*. Take away –ron, and the remaining stem that you can use to form your past-subjunctive conjugations is *habla*. Now, you can add the right ending, choosing either from the –ra or the –se group.

Here are the two groups of conjugations for regular verbs *hablar* (to speak), *vender* (to sell), and *vivir* (to live):

hablara, hablase	*habláramos, hablásemos*
hablaras, hablases	*hablarais, hablaseis*
hablara, hablase	*hablaran, hablasen*

vendiera, vendiese	*vendiéramos, vendiésemos*
vendieras, vendieses	*vendierais, vendieseis*
vendiera, vendiese	*vendieran, vendiesen*

viviera, viviese	*viviéramos, viviésemos*
vivieras, vivieses	*vivierais, vivieseis*
viviera, viviese	*vivieran, viviesen*

Don't forget that if a verb has an irregular preterite *ellos* conjugation, the same irregularity will be retained in the past-subjunctive forms, whether you use –ra or –se endings. For example, the preterite *ellos* form of *querer* (to want) is *quisieron*, so in the past subjunctive the stem of each form should be *quisie–*. Here are the correct conjugations for *querer:*

quisiera, quisiese	*quisiéramos, quisiésemos*
quisieras, quisieses	*quisierais, quisieseis*
quisiera, quisiese	*quisieran, quisiesen*

Using the Past Subjunctive Properly

As its name suggests, the past subjunctive is the past-tense version of the present subjunctive, and the past subjunctive is used in a similar manner–in *que* clauses following a statement of uncertainty, an emotional call, or an expression of need or preference. The only difference is that the main verb that introduces the *que* clause is in the imperfect, preterite, past perfect, or conditional.

Imperfect Tense

As you may remember, the imperfect is used to talk about things that used to happen in the past or that happened over a period of time. Here's how the imperfect may be used with a past-subjunctive clause:

Aquellos días, yo dudaba que mi suerte cambiara.

In those days, I doubted that my luck would change.

Era posible que el maestro no me otorgara el premio.

It was possible that the teacher wouldn't award me with the prize.

Preterite Tense

The preterite is used to describe events at a specific time in the past. Here's an example of how it might work with a past-subjunctive clause:

Cuando vi a mis abuelos, esperé que me trajeran regalos.

When I saw my grandparents, I hoped that they had brought me presents.

En aquel momento me enteré del engaño e insistí que ellos me pidieran perdón.

At that moment, I found out about the deception and insisted that they ask for my forgiveness.

Past Perfect Tense

Past perfect tense is covered in the next chapter. It is a compound tense used to describe that happened before other past-tense events. Here's an example of how the past perfect may be used with a past-subjunctive clause:

Le había dicho a Cristóbal que tuviera cuidado.

I had told Christobal to be careful.

Conditional Tense

One other way of using the past subjunctive is with the conditional tense:

Querríamos que pasearas el perro.

We would like you to walk the dog.

Si pudiera pagar los estudios, me haría piloto.

If I could pay for my studies, I would become a pilot.

FACT

In Spanish, *ojalá que* is an expression meaning "I hope that" or "it's hoped that." You can use the phrase *ojalá que* + past-subjunctive to indicate "I wish that . . . " For example: *Ojalá que ella ganara la lotería.* (I wish she'd win the lottery.)

It's a Command

So far, we've covered two grammatical moods: indicative and subjunctive. The third and final grammatical mood is the imperative mood–the mood of command. Whereas the indicative describes what is and the subjunctive suggests what may be, the imperative mood is used to make a direct address. This is why the imperative mood is basically limited to the second person, "you" *(tú, usted, vosotros, ustedes)*. In Spanish, the imperative mood also works with *nosotros*–in English, it's the equivalent of the phrase "let's."

The mood of command isn't limited to commands, per se. It may be used to ask or even suggest, as long as it's done in a direct address. Here are a few examples of the imperative mood in action:

¡Cállate la boca!

Shut your mouth!

No me mires así.

Don't look at me like that.

Cierra la puerta, por favor.

Please close the door.

No vayamos a la playa hoy—no hace sol.

Let's not go to the beach today—it's not sunny.

Conjugating verbs in the imperative mood is a bit tricky. Some forms look like indicative conjugations, others are identical to subjunctive conjugations, and still others have distinctive endings. Furthermore, the conjugation may change depending on whether the imperative statement is positive (do!) or negative (don't!). The following sections are organized according to the person being addressed–whether you're addressing one or more people, and whether you're using the formal or informal form of address.

Hey, You!

Positive commands directed at *tú* are identical to the third person singular form of the indicative. Compare:

Ella habla inglés. Usted queda en el equipo.

She speaks English. You (formal) are staying on the team.

Habla despacio. Quédate aquí.

Speak slowly. Stay here. (addressed to one person informally)

A few verbs drop the ending in the positive *tú* command:

decir (to say)	*di*
hacer (to do)	*haz*
ir (to go)	*ve*
poner (to put)	*pon*
salir (to leave)	*sal*
ser (to be)	*sé*
tener (to have)	*ten*
venir (to come)	*ven*

The negative form of the *tú* command is rather different: it's identical to the second person singular subjunctive form. Compare the following:

Me alegro que no pierdas tiempo.

I'm happy that you don't waste your time. (informal "you")

No pierdas tiempo.

Don't waste time.

A Formal Address

If the command is addressed to *usted*, the conjugation is identical to the third-person singular of the subjunctive. Similarly, if *ustedes* is the addressee, the conjugation is identical to the third-person plural of the subjunctive. These forms are the same in positive and negative commands.

Por favor, preste atención.

Please pay attention. (to *usted)*

Traigan los libros para la próxima clase.

Bring the books to the next class. (to *ustedes)*

No tire la basura en los lugares públicos.

Don't throw trash in public places. (to *usted)*

To be more polite, add *usted* or *ustedes* to follow the command verb:

Por favor, no entre usted por aquí.

Please do not enter through here.

Let's Do It!

In Spanish, a command may be addressed to *nosotros;* in English, we make these commands with the phrase "let us" or "let's." This kind of a command is still directed at one or more people–it's just that the speaker includes himself or herself in the address.

To form positive and negative commands, you can use the *nosotros* form of the subjunctive:

Escuchemos la música.

Let's listen to music.

No empecemos ya.

Let's not start yet.

Also note that *vamos* is used instead of *vayamos* in positive commands:

Vamos al cine. No vayamos al gimnasio.

Let's go to the movies. Let's not go to the gym.

ALERT

In Spanish, you have the option of making a command indirectly, using the subjunctive mood. For example, instead of saying *mira* ("look" directed at *tú*), you can put it in a more subtle way with *que mires.* Think of it as a shortened form of *yo quiero que mires* (I want you to look).

When in Spain: *Vosotros*

As you know, most people in the Spanish-speaking world will address more than one person with *ustedes*, whether the address is formal or informal. In Spain, there's a distinction between *vosotros* and *ustedes,* and it needs to be retained in the imperative mood.

To make a positive *vosotros* command, drop the final "r" of the verb's infinitive form and replace it with a "d." Take *hablar* as an example: *hablar* – r + d = *hablad.*

Escuchad la música.

Listen to the music.

Desembarcad del tren con cuidado.

Disembark from the train carefully.

The one exception to this rule is the verb *ir* (to go). Instead of *id*, the correct form is *idos:*

Idos a la escuela con nosotros.

Go to the school with us.

To form negative *vosotros* commands, use the *vosotros* subjunctive form:

No prestéis dinero a él.

Don't lend him money.

With Reflexive or Object Pronouns

You've already seen that imperative-mood verbs behave weirdly around subject pronouns–if the pronoun like *tú* or *usted* is there, it follows the verb. There are also some differences in the placement of reflexive and object pronouns. In negative commands, the pronouns behave as usual–they precede the verb. However, in positive commands the pronouns are attached to the end of the verb:

Hazlo como digo.

Do it as I say.

Cuídense bien.

Take care of yourselves.

As a result, some verbs (like *cuidar* in the previous example) require an accent mark to signal correct pronunciation. Furthermore, *nosotros* and *vosotros* forms have a change in the verb ending.

Drop the "S"

In positive *nosotros* commands, the final "s" of the ending is dropped when the verb is combined with the reflexive pronoun *nos* or the indirect object pronoun *se:*

Lavémonos las manos.

Let's wash our hands.

Prestemos el coche a nuestro amigo. Prestémoselo.

Let's lend the car to our friend. Let's lend it to him.

This is done to avoid clunky-sounding forms like *lavémosnos* and *prestémosselo.*

Drop the "D"

Easy pronunciation is also the reason for dropping the "d" in positive *vosotros* commands that end with the reflexive pronoun *os:*

Controlaos, por favor.

Please control yourselves.

Practice Makes Perfect

Conjugate the following verbs (in parentheses) in the present subjunctive:

1. *Ustedes esperan que la profesora* ______________ *(repetir) el trabajo.*
2. *Él no está seguro que su marido* ______________ *(confiarse) en ella.*
3. *Bailamos mientras* ______________ *(tocarse) la música.*
4. *Tú me aconsejas que yo no* ______________ *(pensar) así.*
5. *Estoy lista en caso de que* ______________ *(llegar) temprano.*
6. *Ellos me exigen que yo* ______________ *(fingir) alegría.*
7. *Usted duda que yo* ______________ *(sentirse) bien, ¿verdad?*
8. *Vosotros necesitáis que yo* ______________ *(ser) el médico.*
9. ______________ *(ser) lo que* ______________ *(ser).*

Translate the following commands into Spanish:

1. Open the door! (to *tú)*

   ____
2. Don't stop! (to *vosotros*)

   ____
3. Take my hand! (to *usted)*

   ____
4. Let's go!

   ____
5. Let's not eat it.

   ____

To check your answers, refer to the answer key in Appendix D.

CHAPTER 14

Perfect Compound Tenses

SPANISH TENSES MAY BE DIVIDED into two groups: simple tenses and compound tenses. Simple tenses are verb forms made up of one word–*comprendió* (he understood), *hablaba* (she was talking), *cantarán* (they will sing). Compound tenses are formed with two words–the auxiliary verb that is conjugated to agree with the subject, plus another verb.

You already encountered compound tenses in some of the earlier chapters. Progressive tenses, which use *estar* as the auxiliary verb and the present participle, are used to refer to actions that are happening at a particular time. The perfect tenses make up another important group of compound tenses. Perfect compound tenses describe an action that takes place over time, and it is formed with a conjugated form of *haber* and a past participle.

Haber and Past Participle

Haber is the equivalent of "to have" as used in perfect tenses (not in the sense of owning something); for example, *haber sido* is translated as "to have been." You're already familiar with some forms of *haber* because *haber* is the verb used in the expression "there is/are."

hay	there is/are
hubo	there was/were (preterite)
había	there was/were (imperfect)
habrá	there will be
habría	there would be
haya	there may be (subjunctive)
hubiera	there may have been (past subjunctive)

In compound tenses, *haber* is conjugated to agree in number and person with the subject; the participle form always remains the same.

ESSENTIAL

In Spanish, an adverb cannot be inserted between the auxiliary verb and the main verb. This rule also applies to the compound tenses: *Efectivamente lo he perdido.* (I have really lost it.)

The Past Participle

We've covered past participles in Chapter 9, but let's do a quick review. To form a past participle, choose one of two different endings:

verb group	past participle ending	example
–ar verbs	–ado	*hablado* (spoken)
–er verbs	–ido	*perdido* (lost)
–ir verbs	–ido	*vivido* (lived)

Only a handful of verbs have irregular past participle forms:

abrir	*abierto*	opened
cubrir	*cubierto*	covered
decir	*dicho*	said
escribir	*escrito*	written
hacer	*hecho*	done
ir	*ido*	gone
morir	*muerto*	died
poner	*puesto*	put
romper	*roto*	broken
ser	*sido*	been
ver	*visto*	seen
volver	*vuelto*	returned

Present Perfect

The most common perfect tense is the the present perfect. It's called "present" because it uses the present-tense form of the auxiliary verb *haber*. You are familiar with the English version of this tense—the compound made up of the present form of the verb "to have" and the past participle: "I have done," "she has taken," "they have finished." In English, we use this tense to talk about actions that were done in the recent past and may continue into the present. The same is true for the Spanish equivalent of this tense, *el perfecto de indicativo.*

To form the present perfect, use the present-tense form of the verb *haber*:

he	*hemos*
has	*habéis*
ha	*han*

Le he escrito una carta a Patricio.

I have written a letter to Patricio.

Ellos han preparado una cena para los invitados.

They have prepared a dinner for the guests.

Nosotros nos hemos quejado del mal tiempo.

We have been complaining about the bad weather.

Past-Tense Forms

Since Spanish has two past tenses, preterite and imperfect, it's no surprise that there are also two past perfect compound tenses: past perfect or pluperfect *(pluscuamperfecto)* and preterite perfect *(pretérito anterior o perfecto)*.

Past Perfect: A Past Before the Past

Past perfect tense is used to describe an action that occurred before another past-tense action. In English, the past perfect tense uses the past tense of the verb "to have" plus the participle: "I had done," "she had taken," "they had finished." In Spanish, the imperfect form of the verb *haber* is used. Here's a review of the past-perfect conjugations of *haber:*

había	*habíamos*
habías	*habíais*
había	*habían*

Yo me había levantado antes que ellos me llamaran.

I had gotten up before they called me.

Nosotros habíamos acabado con nuestra cena cuando ella llegó.

We had finished our dinner with she arrived.

Ellos se habían casado antes de que yo los conociera.

They had gotten married before I met them.

Preterite Perfect

The preterite perfect is used much less frequently than the past perfect; generally, you might encounter this tense in literary works (hence it's sometimes known as the literary past tense). The preterite perfect is similar to past perfect, because it refers to actions that had occurred before other actions that took place in the past. However, in the case of the preterite perfect, the action had to have happened just prior to the main event. This is why preterite perfect is generally accompanied by words like *apenas* (scarcely), *en cuanto* (as soon as), and *cuando* (when).

The preterite perfect uses preterite conjugations of the verb *haber* as the auxiliary verb. Here are the conjugations:

hube	*hubimos*
hubiste	*hubisteis*
hubo	*hubieron*

Apenas hube terminado de vestirme cuando ellos llegaron.

I had barely finished getting dressed when they arrived.

En cuanto hubieron llegado a casa, el teléfono empezó a sonar.

As soon as they had gotten home, the phone began to ring.

Future and Conditional

The last two pefect tenses in the indicative mood are the future perfect *(futuro perfecto)* and conditional perfect *(potencial compuesto)*. Both forms are fairly straightforward: Use the future perfect to talk about actions that "will have happened" and the conditional perfect to talk about "what would have happened."

Future Perfect

The future perfect uses the future tense conjugations of *haber*. This compound tense may be used to discuss an event or action that will have happened before another event or action (or before a particular point) in the future.

FACT

The future tense may be used to talk about uncertain events taking place in the present and the conditional tense may apply to uncertain events that took place in the past. The same applies to future perfect and conditional perfect. For example, *yo habré dicho* may mean "I will have said" or "I might have said," depending on context. Similarly, *yo habría dicho* may mean "I would have said" or "I possibly had said."

Here are the future-tense conjugations of *haber*, followed by a few examples:

habré	*habremos*
habrás	*habréis*
habrá	*habrán*

Yo habré terminado el ensayo mañana.

I will have finished the essay by tomorrow.

Ustedes habrán limpiado la mesa antes de salir.

You will have cleaned the table before leaving.

Conditional Perfect

The conditional perfect is used to describe actions that didn't actually take place, but would have, pending a particular condition. Here are the conditional-tense conjugations of the verb *haber:*

habría	*habríamos*
habrías	*habríais*
habría	*habrían*

Si me lo preguntara, yo le habría contestado.

If she had asked me, I would have answered her.

Usted no lo habría hecho, ¿verdad?

You wouldn't have done it, right?

ALERT

Object pronouns always precede the compound verb: *Yo le he dicho a ellos que pueden venir a las siete.* (I have told them that they can come over at seven.) *Ellos lo han hecho ya.* (They have done it already.)

In the Subjunctive

The subjunctive mood also offers two perfect tenses: the present perfect and past perfect. Generally, the rules for using subjunctive in the perfect compound tenses is the same as in the simple tenses.

Present Perfect Subjunctive

Choosing between indicative and subjunctive mood is the same in the present perfect as it is in the present. Use the subjunctive present perfect when the statement expresses opinion, feeling, or attitude, rather than describing real situations. Here are the present-perfect conjugations of *haber:*

haya	*hayamos*
hayas	*hayáis*
haya	*hayan*

Espero que hayas escrito la carta.

I hope you have written the letter.

Necesito hablar con alguien que haya visitado Madrid.

I need to speak with someone who has visited Madrid.

Past Perfect Subjunctive

Similarly, the past perfect subjunctive is used when the main verb of the sentence is in preterite, imperfect, or conditional tense. Here are the past perfect subjunctive conjugations of *haber:*

hubiera	*hubiéramos*
hubieras	*hubierais*
hubiera	*hubieran*

No era cierto que Ramiro y Martín hubieran estado allá.

It wasn't certain that Ramiro and Martin had been there.

Si ellos hubieran estado allá, yo se lo diría a ellos.

If they had been there, I would have told it to them.

Practice Makes Perfect

Fill in the right past participles and translate the sentences into English:

1. *Tú has* ____________ *(acabar) con la cena.*

   ____

2. *Tú habrás* ____________ *(ver) la película antes de la clase mañana.*

   ____

3. *Vosotros vos habíais* ____________ *(levantar) antes que yo llegué aquí.*

   ____

4. *Yo habría* ____________ *(decir) la verdad si me hubieran* ____________ *(preguntar).*

   ____

5. *Hemos* ____________ *(escribir) un ensayo juntos.*

   ____

6. *No era cierto que tú hubieras* ____________ *(ir) por allá.*

   ____

7. *Ellos habían* ____________ *(terminar) sus estudios cuando se apagó la luz.*

   ____

8. *Todos esperan que yo haya* ____________ *(hacer) el trabajo por mí mismo.*

   ____

9. *He* ____________ *(poner) la mochila debajo del escritorio.*

   ____

10. *Ellos han* ____________________ *(ser) estudiantes por muchos años.*

To check your answers, refer to the answer key in Appendix D.

CHAPTER 15

Not to Be Overlooked

WE'RE NOW ALMOST DONE with reviewing parts of speech—nouns, verbs, adjectives, adverbs, and so on. The remaining parts of speech will be covered in this chapter. These include the conjunction, preposition, and interjection. The last section presents a review of affirmative and negative words and phrases (and their correct usage).

In Conjunction

Conjunctions are words that serve a specific grammatical purpose—they help connect single words and phrases within the sentence. Some grammarians subdivide conjunctions into three categories: coordinating, correlative, and subordinating.

Coordinating Conjunctions

Coordinating conjunctions are words that are used to relate like terms, whether each term is a single word or a clause. The most common example of a proper conjunction is *y* (and). You can use *y* to combine a group of nouns, adjectives, or clauses:

Voy a comprar frutas, vegetales y pan.

I'm going to buy fruits, vegetables, and bread.

La película era interesante y divertida.

The movie was interesting and fun.

A mi hermana le gustan los dulces y a mí me gusta el chocolate.

My sister likes candy and I like chocolate.

When *y* precedes a word that begins with a sound *i* (ee), it changes in pronunciation–and spelling–to *e*. For example: *Aprendo castellano e italiano.* (I study Spanish and Italian.) The change has a reasonable explanation: the sound of *e* is different enough from *y* and does not blend in with the beginning of the following word and can be heard distinctly. Another frequently used coordinating conjunction is *o* (or). *O* works similarly to *y*–it may be used to relate single words or clauses:

Me gustaría comer dulces o chocolate.

I would like to eat candy or chocolate.

¿Puede ser o no puede ser?

Could it be or not?

ESSENTIAL

Just as *y* changes to e before words that begin with the sound *i* (ee), the conjunction *o* becomes *u* when it comes before a word that begins with the sound *o*. For example: *Creo que se llama Orlando u Octavio.* (I think his name is Orlando or Octavio.) The explanation here is the same. In conversation, *o* would get lost every time it came before a word that begins with the same sound.

Correlative Conjunctions

Correlative conjunctions come in pairs. In English, these are "either . . . or" and "neither . . . nor," and even native English speakers often have trouble choosing between the two pairs. Here is the basic rule: "Either . . . or" is used in affirmative (positive) sentences–"either one or another." "Neither . . . nor" is only used in negative sentences, when it's "neither one nor the other–none of the two."

In Spanish, use *o . . . o* in the case of "either . . . or" and *ni . . . ni* in the case of "neither . . . nor."

Quisiera o dulces o chocolate.

I would like either candy or chocolate.

No quisiera ni dulces ni chocolate.

I would like neither candy nor chocolate.

In the second example, there's an extra *no* in the Spanish that is dropped in English. That's because Spanish is a language of double negatives. (Double negatives are to be reviewed at the end of this chapter.)

Subordinating Conjunctions

Subordinating conjunctions are used to introduce a dependent clause. You have already seen some examples of how this works from Chapter 13, where the conjunction *que* is used to introduce a clause with a subjunctive mood verb.

Here are some common words that may be used as subordinating conjunctions:

a menos que	unless
a pesar de	despite
aunque	although

cómo	how
con todo	despite, as
cuándo	when
excepto	except
más bien	rather
no obstante	regardless
pero	but
para que	so that
porque	because
que	that
salvo	except
sin embargo	nevertheless
sino	but (following a negative statement)

Pero Versus Sino

In Spanish, there are two different versions of the conjunction "but": *pero* and *sino*. *Sino* is used following a negative clause that is negated to a positive statement. What does that mean? Take a look at the following example:

Ella no tiene un coche, sino una motocicleta.

She doesn't have a car, but (rather) a motorcycle.

In this example, "but" negates a negative, so *sino* is required. In all other situations, you can use the conjunction *pero:*

Ella tiene un coche, pero no tiene motocicleta.

She has a car, but she doesn't have a motorcycle.

Lo siento, pero lo que digo es la verdad.

I'm sorry, but what I'm saying is the truth.

Commonly Used Prepositions

Simply put, a preposition is a word that signals position. In English, "of," "to," for," "from," "in," below, and "above" are common prepositions. As you can see, some prepositions may be used to signal spatial position ("above," "below"), while others ("of" and "for") are more about thc rclation of something to something else.

The preposition generally appears at the helm of the prepositional phrase, which also includes the object of the preposition (a noun or pronoun) plus article and/or adjective. Here are a few examples of what a prepositional phrase is:

inside the yellow box

over the top

behind me

from that foreign country

In Spanish, prepositions work in the same manner, with one caveat. Spanish and English prepositions often don't have a one-to-one correspondence. For example, the preposition *a* may be translated as "to," but it may also be used before direct objects that represent a person or people (as opposed to inanimate objects). Conversely, another word for "to" (as in "toward") in Spanish is *hacia*.

The Versatile A

You can use *a* to indicate direction or movement, as we do in English with the preposition "to":

Vamos a la panadería para comprar galletas.

We are going to the bakery to buy cookies.

Ella corrió al centro para buscar al perro perdido.

She ran downtown to look for the lost dog.

A may also be used to mean "per," "a," or "at" when describing rate or cost:

Hacemos ejercicios tres veces a la semana.

We work out three times a week.

Se venden los zapatos a treinta dólares cada par.

The shoes are on sale for thirty dollars a pair.

This versatile preposition may also be combined with other words to show spatial location. For example, *a la izquierda* and *a la derecha* mean "on the left" and "on the right."

ESSENTIAL

Don't forget that *a* and the definite article *el* (the) combine to form *al*. The same is true of *de* (of, from) and *el:* They combine to form *del*. For example: *Va al banco.* (He is going to the bank.) *Llego del café.* (I'm coming from the café.)

Placed before a direct object, the preposition *a* shows that the direct object is a person–in this case, it is known as the personal *a*. It's important to understand that the personal *a* does not "mean" anything–its only purpose is grammatical. Here are a few examples:

Encontré a Luis en la librería.

I found Luis at the bookstore.

Conozco a aquellos estudiantes;son Silvia y Ramón.

I know those students—they are Silvia and Ramon.

Furthermore, certain verbs may be followed by the preposition *a*, which connects them to another infinitive. For example:

Ayudo a cargar el camión de mudanza.

I am helping to load the moving truck.

Comenzamos a caminar a las siete de la mañana.

We started walking at seven in the morning.

Here are some other verbs commonly paired with the preposition *a:*

acostumbrarse a	to get used to
aprender a	to learn to
apresurarse a	to hurry
atreverse a	to dare to
ayudar a	to help to
comenzar a	to begin to
contribuir a	to contribute to
dedicarse a	to devote oneself to
echarse a	to start to
empezar a	to begin to
enseñar a	to teach how to
invitar a	to invite to
llegar a	to succeed in
negarse a	to refuse

obligar a	to force
prepararse a	to prepare to
ponerse a	to start to
venir a	to come to
volver a	to do again

From, Of, About, and So On

The preposition *de* is generally translated as either "from" or "of," depending on context. Often *de* is used to express ownership. In fact, it replaces the English construction "'s" to show possession:

Esta casa es de los Marín.

That house is the Marin family's.

El cabello de Trina es largo y rubio.

Trina's hair is long and blond.

FACT

In Spanish, you can use *de* in expressions that show a characteristic, like *lleno de* (full of), *vestido de* (dressed in), *pintado de* (painted), and *harto de* (sick of). Another way this can be done is illustrated in the following example: *el hombre de bigotes negros* (the black-moustached man).

The preposition *de* can also be used as the direct equivalent of "of":

Dame un pedazo de pan, por favor.

Give me a piece of bread, please.

"Colombiano" es un adjetivo de nacionalidad.

"Colombian" is an adjective of nationality.

Another way to apply *de* is to mean "made of":

La sopa de frijoles está rica.

The bean soup is delicious.

Mi esposo me regaló un collar de oro.

My husband gave me a gold necklace.

The preposition *de* can also mean "from," when indicating someone's origin or the motion "from" place to place:

Nací en Guatemala. Soy de Guatemala. Soy guatemalteca.

I was born in Guatemala. I am from Guatemala. I am Guatemalan.

Venimos de la oficina del Doctor Fernández.

We're coming from Dr. Fernández's office.

And you can also use *de* in the sense of "about":

Yo sé muy poco de la poesía.

I know very little about poetry.

Es la historia de cómo nos conocimos.

It's the story of (about) how we met.

At, In, On, and More

The preposition *en* is generally equivalent to "in," but it may also be translated as "on" or "at":

Se reunieron en la casa de Pedro.

They gathered at Pedro's house.

Me gusta pasear en el parque.

I like to take walks in the park.

Los niños juegan en la playa.

The kids are playing on the beach.

En is not used to mean "in" in the sense of "inside." For that, use *dentro de:*

Mis padres están dentro de la casa.

My parents are inside the house.

And if you want to say "on" in the sense of "on top of," use *sobre:*

Pon los libros sobre la mesa.

Put the books on the table.

You can also use *en* to mean "by" or "via" (a means by which something is done):

Viajaremos a la Florida en coche.

We'll travel to Florida by car.

With and Without

In Spanish, the preposition equivalent to "with" is *con:*

Prefiero café con leche y dos cucharitas de azúcar.

I prefer my coffee with milk and two teaspoons of sugar.

Tengo ganas de visitar España con mi novio.

I would like to visit Spain with my boyfriend.

ESSENTIAL

When *con* precedes direct object pronouns *mí* (me) or *ti* (you), the preposition and the pronoun combine to form one word: *conmigo* and *contigo.* For example: *Ella fue a la fiesta conmigo.* (She went to the party with me.) *¿Puedo ir contigo?* (Can I come with you?)

Con may also be used to mean "in spite of" or "despite":

Con todos los errores, saqué buena nota en la prueba.

Despite the mistakes, I received a good grade on the quiz.

The opposite of "with" is "without." In Spanish, the equivalent preposition is *sin:*

Ellos viven sin problema.

They live without problems.

Estoy aquí sin Flora porque ella está enferma.

I'm here without Flora because she is ill.

You can also use *sin* to introduce an infinitive verb:

Ella baila sin parar.

She dances non-stop (without stopping).

Por and *Para*

A pair of prepositions that are often misused by students of Spanish, *por* and *para* have similar meanings: *para* may be translated in different contexts as "for," "by," "to," or even "in"; *por* may also mean "in" or "for," or it could mean "on," "through," or "around."

You can use the following rule of thumb to distinguish between the two: *Para* most often means "for": for a cause, for (to) a destination, for someone. And you can think of *por* as "by" or "via"–it's a preposition that describes the way or the instrument by which something was accomplished: by bus, through the woods, in return for your grades.

Now, let's compare the two prepositions:

Vamos para Madrid. Vamos por Madrid.

We're going to Madrid. We're going through Madrid.

In this example, *para* is used to point out the destination, whereas *por* places the travelers in the city. Compare another example:

La carta fue escrita para el gerente. La carta fue escrita por el gerente.

The letter was written for the manager. The letter was written by the manager.

Again, *para* is a preposition that points to someone–the letter is for the manager. *Por*, on the other hand, shows by whom the action is done.

Here are other examples of how *para* can be used:

Para mí, no significa nada.

For me, it doesn't mean anything.

Para un cómico, no es tan gracioso.

For a comedian, he isn't that funny.

Estudio para ser ingeniero.

I study to become an engineer.

Compare that to how *por* may be used:

Por el camino al cine, no encontré nada.

On the way to the movie theater, I didn't find anything.

Vivo aquí por muchos años.

I live here for many years.

Voy a hacerlo por esta razón.

I'm going to do it for this reason.

Compré un reloj por treinta dólares.

I bought a watch for thirty dollars.

Additionally, *por* combines with other prepositions to indicate location:

por encima	over
por detrás	behind
por debajo	under
por acá	around here
por dentro	inside
por fuera	outside

Prepositions of Location

There are quite a few prepositions of location, such us "inside," "near," "next to," and so on.

In Front Of

"In front of" in Spanish is *delante de:*

Hay un árbol delante de la casa.

There is a tree in front of the house.

Facing, Across From

You can use *frente a* and *enfrente de* interchangeably, to mean "facing" or "across from." Here's an example:

La biblioteca está enfrente del restaurante chino.

The library is across from the Chinese restaurant.

Note that it these prepositions may sound like "in front of," but that's *delante de,* not *enfrente de* or *frente a*.

Near and Close By

Cerca de means "near," "close by," or "about":

¿Qué está cerca de la casa de los Smith?

What is near the Smith family's house?

Next To

While *cerca* gives an approximate location, *al lado de* literally means "to the side of" and is used to mean "next to":

El jardín está al lado del río.

The garden is next to the river.

Inside and Outside

The preposition "inside of" is *dentro de* in Spanish and "outside of" is *afuera de*:

Estamos dentro del teatro.

We're inside the theater.

Están afuera del teatro.

They are outside of the theater.

FACT

Sometimes *bajo* is used instead of the longer *debajo. Bajo* is generally used figuratively and does not refer to physical location. For example: *Sirve bajo el Señor de Silva.* (She serves under Señor de Silva.)

Under and Below

The English prepositions "under" and "below" are both translated as *debajo de:*

Los peces nadan debajo de la superficie.

The fish swim below the surface.

Me gusta descansar debajo de los árboles.

I like to rest under the trees.

Behind

In Spanish, the preposition "behind" is *detrás de:*

Creo que está detrás del escritorio.

I think it's behind the desk.

In some cases, *detrás de* may be shortened to *tras,* such as in the expression *año tras año* (year after year).

After Something

When talking about a series of events, you can use *después de* to mean "after":

Voy a verte después de la clase.

I'll see you after class.

Until or Even

The preposition *hasta* can be used to mean "until" or "even":

Estudiaré hasta las once.

I'll study until eleven.

Hasta la profesora no sabe la respuesta.

Not even the teacher knows the answer.

The Rest of the Gang

The rest of the prepositions don't require quite as much explanation. Most of them only have one equivalent translation in English.

Before

Antes de and *antes que* mean "before" when talking about time. Compare the following:

La cena terminó antes de su llegada.

Dinner ended before his arrival.

La cena terminó antes que llegara.

Dinner ended before he arrived.

As you can see, *antes de* is used before a noun *llegada* and *antes que* is used before a verb *llegara.*

Against

Contra and the longer form, *en contra de* (used in expressions that refer to taking a stand against an idea) are translated as "against":

Yo estoy en contra de los ideas comunistas.

I am against communist ideas.

Ella está parada contra la pared.

She is standing against the wall.

A Sign of Excitement

The interjection, *la interjección,* is a part of speech that isn't used very frequently, even though it is very expressive. Any word that is used solely to express a state of excitement or another emotion is an interjection. Common interjections in English are: Wow! No way! Sheesh! Hey, there! Huh!

Some interjections are made up of exclamation words that don't have any other meaning:

¡ah!	ah! ha! oh! (surprise)
¡ay!	ouch! oh, dear! (pain, sorrow)
¡bah!	Phooey! (disbelief)
¡eh!	hey! (getting attention)
¡huy!	ow! (pain) wow! (amazement) jeez! (surprise) phew! (relief)
¡oh!	oh! (surprise, admiration, sorrow, happiness, etc.)
¡olé!	bravo!
¡puf!	ugh!
¡uf!	phew! (tiredness)

Other interjections may incorporate words and phrases that actually do have some meaning. Here are a few common interjections in Spanish:

¡calla!	be quiet!
¡despacio!	slow down!
¡dios mío!	my God!
¡hombre!	man!
¡qué!	what!
¡qué pena!	what a pity!
¡vaya!	let's go!

 **ESSENTIAL**

Don't forget that in Spanish, an exclamation (whether it's a word or a phrase) must be enclosed in two exclamation marks, the first of which is upside down: *¡ay!* Double exclamation marks work on the same principle as quotation mark pairs. Just as you would use quotation marks to enclose a word or phrase quoted, use the exclamation marks to enclose the exclamation.

The Case of Double Negatives

The most important point to remember about the Spanish negatives is that double negatives are a must. This is difficult to understand for speakers of English, because double negatives in our language are a grammatical no-no. Compare the following sentence in Spanish and English:

Nosotros no vemos nada.

We don't see anything. (We see nothing.)

In Spanish, you need to emphasize *no* with a second negative, *nada* (nothing). In English, you would use either "no" or "nothing," but you can't have both in the same phrase. Also note the placement of *no*—it is always placed before the verb and following the subject, if one is present.

In Time

Affirmative and negative words and expressions regarding time are:

nunca	never
jamás	never
ninguna vez	never once
alguna vez	once, sometime
algunas veces	sometimes
a veces	sometimes
otra vez	again
muchas veces	often
a menudo	often
siempre	always

No lo hago nunca.

I never do it.

Lo hago algunas veces.

I do it sometimes.

Siempre lo hago.

I always do it.

People and Things

Affirmatives and negatives work similarly with words referring to people or things, but don't forget to use the personal *a* before *alguien* and *nadie*.

nada	nothing
nadie	no one
alguien	someone, somebody
algo	something
todo	everything
todos	everybody

Necesito algo. Necesito todo.

I need something. I need everything.

No conozco a nadie aquí.

I don't know anyone here.

Los conozco a todos aquí.

I know everyone here.

ESSENTIAL

Don't forget about affirmative and negative adjectives *ninguno* and *alguno,* and that they must agree in gender and number with the noun they modify: *ningún hombre* (no man); *algunas cosas* (some things).

On Location

Whereas in English there are words like "nowhere" and "somewhere," in Spanish you'll need to use expressions that mean "at no part" or "in some parts":

por/en ninguna parte	nowhere
por/en ningún lado	nowhere
por/en alguna parte	somewhere
por/en algún lado	somewhere
por/en todas partes	everywhere

No lo puedo encontrar por ninguna parte.

I can't find him anywhere.

Debe estar en algún lado.

He must be somewhere.

Other Words and Expressions

There are a few other negatives and affirmatives that are worth reviewing. Let's start with *tampoco* (either/neither) and *también* (also, too). If you think about it, these two words are a negative and positive equivalent of the same idea. Compare the following:

Tampoco sabe lo que pasó.

He doesn't know what happened either.

También sabe lo que pasó.

He knows what happened too.

In these examples, *tampoco* and *también* are both used to mean "also" or "as well," but in the case of *tampoco,* the agreement is in a negative context–no one knows what happened and he doesn't know what happened either.

Also compare *ni/ni* (neither nor) and *o/o* (either or):

No conozco ni a Silvia ni a Alejandro.

I know neither Silvia nor Alejandro.

(I don't know either Silvia or Alejandro)

Conozco o a Silvia o a Alejandro.

I know either Silvia or Alejandro.

As you can see, if the statement is negative, in Spanish you would use *ni/ni* even if the English translation is either/or.

Practice Makes Perfect

Translate the following sentences into Spanish:

1. I'd like to either play soccer or swim in the sea.

____

2. He doesn't want either carrots or onions in his salad.

____

3. They neither want to stay home or go to the beach.

____

4. Neither he nor she wants to come with us.

____

5. I don't have pencils, but (I do have) pens.

____

6. Although she feels tired, she'll get together with the team.

____

7. Despite everything that's happening, we are fine.

____

8. Nevertheless, you (plural) are happy to be here.

____

Insert *por* and *para* where necessary:

1. *Voy a la playa* ____________ *nadar en el mar.*
2. *Van al mercado* ____________ *autobús.*
3. *Nos gusta pasear* ____________ *las calles de la ciudad.*
4. *La cena fue preparada* ____________ *mí; yo la preparé.*
5. *La carpeta con la información está* ____________ *dentro.*
6. *Hoy es tu cumpleaños. Este regalo es* ____________ *ti.*
7. *He trabajado en la oficina* ____________ *muchos años.*
8. *¿* ____________ *qué es así?*

To check your answers, refer to the answer key in Appendix D.

CHAPTER 16

Questions and Answers

BY NOW YOU SHOULD BE comfortable with the order of words in the Spanish sentence. Generally it goes like this: subject + object pronouns (if any) + verb + object. Now, be prepared for a shift. In Spanish (just as in English), the order of words may change when you form a question.

I Have a Question

Asking questions in Spanish isn't very different from how we do it in English—but you probably never even thought about how it's done in English and did it automatically. Now you'll have to pay attention. To form a question in Spanish, there are four basic options:

1. Raising your voice at the end of the sentence.
2. Inverting the subject and verb.
3. Adding a question phrase at the end of the statement.
4. Using a question word.

The first option is simplest. As you ask the following question, your voice should rise by the time you get to "ña" in *mañana*:

¿El electricista llega mañana?

The electrician will come tomorrow?

Don't forget that in Spanish, question marks work just like quotation marks: You need two of them to frame the question, and the first question mark looks like it's upside down. Here are two examples: *¿Qué quieres hacer hoy?* (What do you want to do today?) *Quieres ir a compras, ¿verdad?* (You want to go shopping, right?)

To emphasize what you're asking, you can also invert the subject and verb of the sentence. In the following example, the subject *tú* and the verb *eres* switch places:

¿Eres tú la actriz del teatro Colón en Argentina?

Are you the actress from the Colon theater in Argentina?

It's also possible to turn a statement into a question by adding a question word or phrase to the end of it:

Están de acuerdo conmigo, ¿verdad?

You agree with me, right?

Hoy es miércoles, ¿no es así?

Today is Wednesday, isn't it?

Other question words and phrases that may be added to the end of statements include the following:

¿no es cierto?	isn't it certain?
¿no?	or not?
¿sí?	right?
¿eh?	huh? (waiting for confirmation)

ESSENTIAL

In Spanish, it's not possible to add a question to the end of a statement by repeating the pronoun and verb in the negative ("isn't he?" "aren't we?" "don't you?" and so on). These can all be translated into Spanish with a generic question phrase like *¿no es así?*

And, finally, you can ask questions by using question words like *¿qué?* (what?), *¿cómo?* (how?), *¿cuándo?* (when?), *¿dónde?* (where?), *¿cuál?* (which), and *¿quién?* (who?).

¿Dónde está la florería?

Where is the florist's shop located?

¿Quién es la chica con los pantalones blancos?

Who is the girl in white pants?

Yes, No, or Maybe

For the first three groups of questions, the expected answer may be *sí* (yes), *no* (no), or any of the words we might translate as "maybe": *quizá* (or *quizás*), *tal vez,* and *a lo mejor.* Another way of saying "maybe" is with a verb phrase–*puede que* or *puede ser que.* Note that the clause the follows will be in the subjunctive mood.

Let's look at some examples of questions and answers. Let's say the question is:

¿Es Londres la capital de Inglaterra?

Is London the capital of England?

Here are some appropriate responses:

Sí, Londres es la capital de Inglaterra.

Yes, London is the capital of England.

No, Londres no es la capital de Inglaterra. Es la capital del Reino Unido.

No, London isn't the capital of England. It's the capital of the United Kingdom.

FACT

Many of the question words also have non-question meanings. For example, *que* means "that" and *para que* means "so that." In Spanish writing, the question words are distinguished with the use of an accent mark. For example, *qué* means "what?" and *que* is "that."

Tal vez Londres es la capital de Inglaterra, no estoy seguro.

Maybe London is the capital of England, I'm not sure.

No sé. Quizás París es la capital de Inglaterra.

I don't know. Maybe Paris is the capital of England.

Puede ser que Londres sea la capital de Inglaterra.

Maybe (it's possible) that London is the capital of England.

Question Words

Journalists are taught that to write a good story, they must answer the five W questions: who, what, where, when, and why. Let's get acquainted with the Spanish question words (also known as interrogatives) that are the equivalent of these, plus a few others.

Qué—What's Going On?

To ask "what?" use the question word *¿qué?*

¿Qué es esto?

What is this?

¿Qué tipo de corte de pelo prefieres?

What type of haircut do you prefer?

¿Qué? may be used in conjunction with a preposition:

¿con qué?	how? with what?
¿de qué?	of what? from what?
¿para qué?	why? for what purpose?
¿por qué?	why?

In Spanish there's no separate word for "why?" Instead, you can use either *¿para qué?* or *¿por qué?* The first of the two is used to ask "for what purpose?" while the second one is a more traditional form of "why?" Compare:

¿Para qué estás aquí?

Why are you here? (For what purpose are you here?)

¿Por qué estás aquí?

Why are you here? (What's the reason?)

Quién—Look Who's Talking

There are two forms of the question "who?" in Spanish: *¿quién?* (singular) and *¿quiénes?* (plural):

¿Quién es el presidente de los Estados Unidos?

Who is the president of the United States?

¿Quiénes son los líderes del equipo?

Who are the team leaders?

ESSENTIAL

Just as "why" is really a combination of "for" and "what" *(¿por qué?),* "whose" is a combination of "of" and "who" *(¿de quién?).* Since Spanish doesn't form possessives with 's, the answer to the question *¿de quién?* is always *de* + possessor: *¿De quién son estos libros? Esos libros son de María.* (Whose books are these? Those books are Maria's.)

Other question words based on *¿quién?* and *¿quiénes?* are:

¿a quién?	whom? (singular)
¿a quiénes?	whom? (plural)
¿con quién?	with whom? (singular)
¿con quiénes?	with whom? (plural)
¿de quién?	whose? (singular)
¿de quiénes?	whose? (plural)

¿A quién debo contactar para conseguir la información?

Whom should I contact to get the information?

¿De quiénes son estos libros?

Whose books are these?

Dónde—Where It's At

The question "where?" is *¿dónde?* in Spanish. This question word is used to ask about location of a person or thing and is often used with the verb *estar* (to be):

¿Dónde están los zapatos rojos de tacón alto?

Where are the red high-heeled shoes?

When the verb of the question is a verb of motion, like *ir* (to go) or *caminar* (to walk), use the question word *¿adónde?* (to where?):

¿Adónde van los chicos?

Where are the boys going?

¿Adónde camina aquella gente?

Where are those people walking?

In *adónde,* the *a* represents "to," so the questions in the last examples are really "To where are the boys going?" and "To where are those people walking?" Other question phrases that may be formed with *dónde* are:

¿de dónde?	from where?
¿hacia dónde?	toward where?
¿para dónde?	toward where?

Cuánto—How Much and How Many

In English, there are two question phrases that may be used when asking about quantity. If you're asking about quantifiable things (things that you can count, like apples or chairs or doctors), the right question is "how many?" If you're asking about unquantifiable things (water, money, time), you'll ask "how much?"

In Spanish, both questions are translated as variants *¿cuánto?* If you mean "how many?" the question word is plural and must agree with the gender of the objects being counted. That means you've got two options: *¿cuántos?* and *¿cuántas?* If the question is "how much," the question word has to be in its singular form, so the two options are *¿cuánto?* and *¿cuánta?*

Here are a few examples:

¿Cuánto tiempo tienes para mí?

How much time do you have for me?

¿Cuánta energía tienes para continuar?

How much energy do you have to continue?

¿Cuántos amigos te visitaron?

How many friends visited you?

¿Cuántas muñecas tienes para jugar?

How many dolls do you have to play with?

In the previous examples, the question word *cuánto* was used as an adjective–it modified *tiempo, energía, amigos,* and *muñecas.* But *cuánto* can also be used on its own as a pronoun:

¿Cuánto cuestan los tomates?

How much are the tomatoes?

In this case, *cuánto* is not the adjective of *dinero* (money)–instead, it replaces it.

ALERT

When *cuánto* is used as a pronoun, it does not have to reflect the gender and number of the noun it replaces—regardless of the thing or things being asked about, it always retains the –o ending.

Cuál—Which Is It, Anyway?

"Which?" in Spanish has two versions, a singular and a plural: *¿cuál?* and *¿cuáles?* However, *cuál/cuáles* and "which" aren't necessarily equivalent. When "which?" is used as an adjective before a noun, the correct translation is *¿qué?*

¿Qué tipo de tela prefieres?

Which kind of fabric do you prefer?

¿Qué frutas te gusta comer?

Which fruit do you like to eat?

On the other hand, sometimes *cuál/cuáles* is needed when a good English translation calls for "what?"

¿Cuál es la fecha de hoy?

What (which) day is it today?

¿Cuál es la capital de Perú?

What is the capital of Peru?

Cómo and *Cuándo*—How and When

The last two question words are relatively simple–both *¿cómo?* and *¿cuándo?* have a direct equivalent in English: "how" and "when," respectively.

¿Cómo se dice "Irlanda" en inglés?

How do you say *Irlanda* in English?

¿Cuándo regresará mamá?

When will mom come back?

What Time Is It?

Asking about time is a frequent kind of question, and it deserves some attention. In Spanish, the word for "time" is *tiempo.*

¿Qué hora es?

What time is it?

Literally, the question is "What hour is it?" In the answer, the word *hora* is dropped, but it affects the conjugation of the verb and the gender of the definite article *la/las:*

Es la una.

It's one o'clock.

Son las dos.

It's two o'clock.

Son las once.

It's eleven o'clock.

QUESTION?

What about a.m. and p.m.?
In Spanish, the twenty-four hours are divided into morning, afternoon, and night. From 1 a.m. until 11 a.m., use *de la mañana;* from 1 p.m. until around 7 or 8 p.m. you can say *de la tarde;* the rest of the time, the right phrase is *de la noche.*

To Be More Specific

Let's review the phrases for giving more exact times. If it's a few minutes past the hour, simply use *y* (and) to add the minutes:

Son las cuatro y diez de la tarde.

It's ten minutes past four in the afternoon (4:10 P.M.).

If it's just a few minutes before the hour, you can either add the minutes or you may round up with the help of the word *menos* (minus):

Son las cuatro y cincuenta.

It's four fifty (4:50).

Son las cinco menos diez.

It's ten minutes to five.

And here are additional options for saying 4:15, 4:30, and 4:45:

Son las cuatro y cuarto.

It's four and a quarter (4:15).

Son las cuatro y media.

It's four and a half (4:30).

Son las cinco menos cuarto.

It's a quarter to five (4:45).

The following examples contain phrases associated with noon and midnight:

Son las doce de la noche. Es medianoche.

It's twelve at night. It's midnight.

Son las doce del día. Es mediodía.

It's twelve noon. It's noontime.

Other Frequently Asked Questions

Now that we've reviewed the basic question formats and the question words, let's end the chapter with a review of frequently asked questions.

¿Cómo te llamas? ¿Cómo se llama?

What's your name? (informal and formal)

¿Cuál es la fecha de hoy?

What day is it today?

¿Cuánto cuesta el pan? ¿Cuánto cuestan las piñas?

How much is the bread? How much are the pineapples?

¿Cúantos años tienes? ¿Cuántos años tiene usted?

How old are you? (informal and formal)

¿Qué significa esto?

What does this mean?

¿Me entiendes? ¿Me entiende?

Do you understand me? (informal and formal)

If you didn't understand the answer, you can say *¿Cómo?* (What?) to clarify.

Practice Makes Perfect

Answer the following questions:

1. *¿Es Bogotá la capital de Colombia?*

   ____

2. *¿Qué vas a hacer hoy?*

   ____

3. *¿De qué color es tu cabello?*

   ____

4. *¿Por qué estudias este idioma?*

   ____

5. *¿Quién era el presidente de los Estados Unidos durante la Guerra Civil?*

   ____

6. *¿De quién es este libro?*

   ____

7. *¿Con quiénes te gustaría viajar a España?*

8. *¿Dónde vives?*

9. *¿Adónde vas de vacaciones?*

10. *¿Cuánto cuesta este libro?*

11. *¿Cuántos hermanos tienes?*

12. *¿Cuál es la fecha de hoy?*

13. *¿Cuál es la capital de Francia?*

14. *¿Cómo se dice "generous" en español?*

15. *¿Cuándo empezaste a estudiar español?*

To check your answers, refer to the answer key in Appendix D.

CHAPTER 17

Building Vocabulary

THE MOST OBVIOUS WAY TO IMPROVE your Spanish vocabulary is through memorization and practice. You cannot avoid memorizing words–it's the only sure way of increasing your vocabulary, and you won't be able to assimilate these words if you don't practice using them. However, additional strategies are available to you as well. For instance, by learning the meanings of common prefixes and suffixes, you'll be able to understand many more words than you have committed to memory. If you know that cantar means "to sing," and you know that -ción is a suffix equivalent to the English "-tion" and may be used to turn verbs into nouns, you might be able to guess that canción means "song."

The Structure of a Spanish Word

A Spanish word may be made up of one or two parts–a lexeme (*lexema)* and/or a morpheme (*morfema).* The lexeme is the word's basic meaning, so it is generally the word's root. For example, take the following words:

cocina	kitchen
cocinar	to cook
cocinero	cook, chef
cocineta	kitchenette
precocinado	precooked

These five words share the root *-cocin-*, a lexeme that conveys the meaning of "cooking." The particles -a, -ar, -ero, -eta, pre-, and -ado (a prefix and five suffixes) may be called morphemes—they don't have a meaning on their own but do add meaning when presented together with the root.

ESSENTIAL

Endings that are used to show agreement and tense—like *-án* in *cantarán* (they will sing) or *-s* in *pedazos* (pieces)—are not morfemes. For example, in the word *cocineros*, *cocin-* is a lexeme of meaning, *-ero* is a suffix, and *-s* is an ending.

You can use lexemes and morphemes to your advantage. For example, once you understand that *cocin* is a root that has to do with cooking, you'll be able to guess the meaning of other words with the same lexeme, such as *cocido* (cooked) and *recocido* (overcooked)—as long as you are familiar with the prefix *re-* (over-) and suffix *-ido* (-ed).

Presenting the Prefix

A prefix *(prefijo)* is a morpheme that is attached to the front end of a word. In the word "prefix," for example, the prefix is "pre-." In Spanish *prefijo*, the prefix is the same: *pre-*. The following list of Spanish prefixes is by no means complete, but it does include the more commonly used prefixes.

- **a-** deprivation or negation; may have other meanings

ateísmo	atheism, rejection of theism
acabar	to end, to finish
atraer	to attract

- **ante–** previously, beforehand, pre-, fore-

anteayer	day before yesterday
antemano	beforehand
antebrazo	forearm

- **anti–** a prefix of opposition, anti-

antinatural	unnatural
antipatía	antipathy
antisudoral	antiperspirant

- **auto–** self-, auto-, by oneself

autobiografía	autobiography, a biography of one's own life
autodefensa	self-defense
autorización	authorization

- **contra–** a prefix of opposition

contracubierta	back cover
contragolpe	counter-blow
contrapelo	against the grain, the wrong way; literally "against the hair"

- **con–** (also **con–** or **co–**) a prefix of addition or association

conmover	to move, to touch
consagrar	to consecrate
consorte	consort, accomplice
compadecer	to sympathize with
coautor	coauthor

- **de–** (also **des–**) downward motion, separation, origin, opposite of the root meaning, emphasis

descender	to descend
denuncio	denunciation
derivar	to derive from
decolorado	discolored
demandar	to demand
desabrochar	to undo

ALERT

You may have noticed that some prefixes have the same or a similar meaning in English and in Spanish. That's because these prefixes have the same origin—they've come to us from Latin or Greek. However, be aware that some prefixes may look the same but don't necessarily have the same meanings.

- **en–** (**em–** before "b" or "p") inside, on the interior; the prefix of connecting, enclosing

enlazar	to link
enmicar	to cover in plastic
embarazo	pregnancy

- **ex–** outside of, further (over space or time); may not have a specific meaning

extraer	extract, draw
expansivo	expansive
explicar	to explain

- **extra–** over, outside of, exceedingly

extrafino	superfine
extranjero	foreigner, outsider
extraño	strange

- **in–** (**im–** before "b" or "p"; **i–** before "l" or "r") inside, on the interior; may carry a meaning of deprivation

incluir	to include
inacción	inaction
importante	important
iletrado	illiterate, uneducated

- **inter–** between, among

internacional	international, among nations
interactivo	interactive
interesado	interested

- **para–** with, to the side of, against

paradoja	paradox
parafrasear	to paraphrase
parasitario	parasitic

- **per–** a prefix of intensity; may signify "badly"

perjurar	to perjure
pertinencia	relevance
pervivir	to survive

- **pre–** prior to, priority, beforehand

pretexto	pretext
prevenido	cautious
previsión	foresight

- **pro–** by or instead of, before, moving forward, denial or contradiction, in favor of

pronombre	pronoun
prólogo	prologue
propulsar	to drive, propel
proclamar	to proclaim
proponer	to propose

- **re–** repetition, moving backwards, intensification, opposition

reeligir	to re-elect
recapacitar	to reconsider
recargar	to refill
rechazar	to refuse

FACT

In addition to prefixes and suffixes, Spanish also has infixes. The infix is a morpheme that can only appear between the root and the suffix. How can you tell the difference between a suffix and an infix? The root + infix do not make a complete word. For example, in the word *jardinería* (gardening), –ia is an suffix but –er– is an infix—*jardiner* is not a real word in Spanish.

- **sub-** below; may also indicate inferiority

subarrendar	to sublet
subcutáneo	subcutaneous, under the skin
subempleo	underemployment

- **uni-** one, alone

unido	united
universal	universal
unívoco	one to one

Following with the Suffix

A suffix *(sufijo)* is a morpheme that is attached to the end of a root. Suffixes often establish the word's grammatical role in the sentence—whether it's a noun, verb, or adjective: *divertirse* (to have fun), *diversión* (fun, a hobby), *divertido* (fun). The following list includes the more commonly used suffixes—knowing these suffixes can help you figure out the meanings of words you're not familiar with—or you can even try creating new words yourself.

- **-aje** forms a noun from another noun; English equivalents are -ship and -age

aprendizaje	apprenticeship
caudillaje	leadership
kilometraje	"mileage" (for kilometers)

- **-ancia** a suffix that forms nouns; direct English equivalent is -ancy

corpulencia	stoutness
tolerancia	tolerance
violencia	violence

- **–anza** forms a noun, often from a verb; English equivalents include –ance, –ion, and –ity

enseñanza	education
semejanza	similarity
venganza	vengeance

- **–ario** a noun suffix that indicates a profession or place; English equivalents are –er, –ian, and –ry

bancario	banker
bibliotecario	librarian
campanario	bell tower

- **–arquía** a suffix meaning "rule" or "government"; the English equivalent is –archy

anarquía	anarchy
jerarquía	hierarchy
monarquía	monarchy

- **–ble** this suffix forms adjectives; it plays the same role in Spanish as it does in English

deseable	desirable
increíble	incredible
manejable	manageable

- **–cida/-cidio** another noun suffix meaning "killing"; direct English equivalent is the suffix –cide

homicidio	homicide
insecticida	insecticide
suicidio	suicide

- **–ción** a noun suffix; its direct English equivalent is –tion

información	information
presentación	presentation
culminación	culmination, end result

- **–dad** This suffix often turns an adjective into a noun; the English equivalents are –ty and –hood

hermandad	brotherhood
lealdad	loyalty
verdad	truth

FACT

Alternate forms of *–dad* suffix are *–idad*, *–edad,* and *–eidad*. Examples: *hosquedad* (gloominess), *comunidad* (community), and *simplicidad* (simplicity).

- **–ear** a suffix that helps turn a noun into a verb

deletrear	to spell
parpadear	to blink
pasear	to stroll, take a walk

- **–ense** a suffix that is added to a country's name to create the adjective of nationality

canadiense	Canadian
costarriquence	Costa Rican
rioplatense	from the Rio Plata region in South America

- **-ería** a noun suffix indicating a place (often a shop)

lavandería	laundromat
panadería	bakery
zapatería	shoe store

- **-ero/-era** may indicate a profession or role; English equivalents include -er and -or

ingeniero	engineer
traicionero	traitor
portero	doorman

- **-esa/-iz/-isa** indicates profession in the feminine; English equivalent is -ess

actriz	actress
duquesa	duchess
poetisa	poetess

- **-eza** a suffix used to turn an adjective into a noun; an English equivalent is -ty

belleza	beauty
pureza	purity
riqueza	riches, wealth

- **-icio/-icia** a noun suffix; English equivalent is -ice

avaricia	avarice
novicio	novice
justicia	justice

- **–ificar** a suffix that forms verbs and means turn into"; English equivalent is –ify

dignificar	to dignify
dosificar	to measure out (dose)
significar	to mean

- **–ismo** a noun suffix that refers to a "theory" or "ideology"; English equivalent is –ism

comunismo	communism
racismo	racism
realismo	realism

- **–ista** a noun suffix that is often used to indicate profession or role; English equivalent is –ist

comunista	communist
dentista	dentist
pianista	pianist

- **–izo** an adjective suffix that connotes uncertainty or incompleteness of a quality (English equivalent is –ish); signals what something is made of

cobrizo	coppery
pajizo	made of straw
rojizo	reddish

- **–mente** a common suffix used to turn an adjective into an adverb; English equivalent is –ly

claramente	clearly
obviamente	obviously
precisamente	precisely

- **–or** a noun suffix that is often used to represent a profession or role; English equivalents include –er and –or

director	director, editor, headmaster, manager
jugador	player
pintor	painter

- **–oso** a suffix you can use to turn a noun into an adjective; English equivalent is –ous

jugoso	juicy
maravilloso	marvelous
peligroso	dangerous

- **–tud** a noun suffix that often refers to a state of being; English equivalent is –ude

actitud	attitude
latitud	latitude
solicitud	solicitude

ESSENTIAL

Don't forget that while a suffix like –or is used to create profession words, you still need to add the right endings if the person described is female, or if there is more than one person: *jugador, jugadora, jugadores, jugadoras.*

Diminutives and Augmentatives

There are two groups of suffixes that deserve special attention—they are the suffixes that form diminutives and augmentatives. These are suffixes that can be added to a whole range of words and the resulting words don't require a dictionary definition—the suffixes don't change the word's meaning, they simply signal additional information like size or the speaker's emotional attitude.

Diminutive—Small

"Diminutive" means "small"; diminutive suffixes indicate small size, cuteness, or the attitude of endearment. The word *caja* means "box"; *cajita* is a little box, perhaps one of those ring boxes. *Perro* is a dog; *perrito* is "doggy." As you can see, using a diminutive suffix can allow you to be more descriptive without resorting to adjectives.

The most versatile diminutive suffix in Spanish is *–ito* and its conjugated forms, *–ita, –itos,* and *–itas: conejito* (little bunny), *abuelita* (granny), *chiquitos* (little/cute boys), *abejitas* (litte/cute bees). Here are a few other diminutive suffixes commonly used in Spanish:

–cito (–cita)	*ratoncito*	little mouse
–illo (–illa)	*chiquillo*	little boy
–zuelo (–zuela)	*jovenzuelo*	youth

You can take almost any noun and give it a diminutive suffix. Even adjectives and, to a lesser extension, adverbs can take on diminutive endings: *viejito* (old), *rapidito* (quickly). However, be aware that diminutives are often considered "slangy" and should not be overused in writing or in formal speech.

QUESTION?

Do diminutives exist in English as well?
They do, although they are not as common. You've already seen the example of "dog" and "doggy." Another suffix that forms diminutives is –y and variant forms like –sy: compare "cute" and "cutesy."

Augmentative—Large

The word "augmentative" means "enlarging" (to augment is to enlarge). Augmentatives are similar to diminutives, except that their endings carry a different tone—they indicate large size or the attitude of toughness or importance. For example, *hombre* is "man," but add the augmentative suffix *-ón*, and the result is *hombrón*, "tough guy." Here's a list of common augmentative suffixes:

–ote (–ota)	*grandote*	very big
–ón (–ona)	*barracón*	a big hut
–azo (–aza)	*buenazo*	really good

 **FACT**

Technically, there's a third group of suffixes in the diminutive/augmentative club: the pejoratives. Basically, a pejorative ending will turn a word into an insult. Pejorative endings include *–aco*, *–aca*, *–acho*, *–acha*, *–ajo*, *–aja*, *–ote*, *–ota*, *–ucho*, and *–ucha*.

Recognizing Cognates

Another way to improve your vocabulary is by learning how to recognize cognates—word pairs that look alike or are very similar in English and in Spanish. True cognates are cognates that also share a common or very similar meaning. For example, compare "attention" and *atención*—these two words have a similar spelling and share a similar meaning. And *exterior* is identical to the English "exterior."

In the case of some Spanish cognates, it's easy to see what they could mean in English. For example, if you encounter the word *cliente*, you'll likely be able to guess that it's a cognate of "client." Likewise, *imposible* looks very much like "impossible," though it's pronounced slightly differently (the "e" isn't silent).

Other cognate pairs aren't as obvious, however, and you'll need to practice guessing to be able to figure out the correct meaning. For example, it may not be immediately clear that *traducción* is the Spanish cognate of "translation" or that *estudiar* is a cognate for "to study."

Furthermore, some simple Spanish words have English cognates that we would consider old-fashioned words or even "vocabulary" words. Compare the following:

aumentar	to augment (to increase)
discordia	discord (disagreement)
escolástico	scholastic (academic, scholarly)
penúltimo	penultimate (second to last)
serpiente	serpent (snake)

One important benefit of learning these cognates is that you'll also improve your English vocabulary.

Commonly Misused Cognates

Although paying attention is to your advantage, it's important to keep in mind that not all cognates are true cognates—that is, not all cognates actually have a common or similar meaning in English and Spanish. Many a student of Spanish has been mortified to learn that *embarazada* means "pregnant" and not "embarrassed," as may be concluded. "Embarrassed" and *embarazada* are just one pair of false cognates. The following tables lists a few others.

Spanish	Correct English Translation	False Cognate	Correct Spanish Translation
asistir	to attend	to assist	*ayudar*
atender	to serve	to attend	*asistir*
billón	trillion	billion	*mil millones*
campo	field, countryside	camp	*campamento, facción*
chocar	to crash	to choke	*ahogar, sofocar*
colegio	school	college	*escuela universitaria, universidad*
compromiso	obligation, commitment	compromise	*arreglo, solución*
constiparse	to catch a cold	to be constipated	*estar extreñido*
desgracia	misfortune	disgrace	*deshonra*
educado	well-mannered, polite	educated	*culto*
embarazada	pregnant	embarrassed	*avergonzado*
emocionante	thrilling, moving	emotional	*emocional*
éxito	success	exit	*salida*
fábrica	factory	fabric	*tela*
firma	signature	firm	*compañía*
idioma	language	idiom	*modismo*
largo	long	large	*grande*
librería	bookstore	library	*biblioteca*
molestar	to bother	to molest	*agredir sexualmente*
pretender	to try, to hope to achieve	to pretend	*fingir, similar*
raro	strange	rare	*excepcional, poco común*
realizar	to actualize	to realize	*darse cuenta*
ropa	clothing	rope	*cuerda*
sano	healthy	sane	*cuerdo, sabio*
sensible	sensitive	sensible	*razonable, sensato*
sopa	soup	soap	*jabón*
suceso	event	success	*éxito*
vaso	drinking glass	vase	*jarrón*

Chapter 18

Writing in Spanish

PART OF BEING PROFICIENT in a language is being able to write in it. This means being able to spell correctly, knowing the rules of capitalization and punctuation, and knowing how to proofread your work—dotting the i's and crossing the t's, so to speak.

Don't Overcapitalize

Overall, the rules of capitalization are very similar in English and in Spanish. Capitalization is used in three basic ways:

1. To indicate the beginning of a sentence.
2. To distinguish proper names.
3. In titles of books, movies, lectures, and so on; in headers.

QUESTION?

What is a "proper name"?
A proper name is what something or someone is named, as opposed to what it is. In the following pairs, the first is a proper name: John/boy, Barcelona/city, Mrs. MacDuff/teacher, and so on.

The first rule should be pretty clear. Be sure to capitalize the first word of every new sentence, just as you do in English.

Proper Names

The second rule, which deals with proper names, is also pretty similar in English and in Spanish. Names of people, cities, and countries are capitalized in both languages:

Me llamo Benicio Juan Armandez.

My name is Benicio Juan Armandez.

Vivo en Buenos Aires, la capital de Argentina.

I live in Buenos Aires, the capital of Argentina.

Brand names are also considered proper names:

Prefiero las zapatillas de deportes marca Nike.

I prefer Nike sneakers.

Titles and Headers

However, the third rule of capitalization isn't exactly identical in English and Spanish. In English, we generally capitalize most of the words in a title or header (the exceptions being prepositions shorter than six letters and articles, although these rules may vary). In Spanish, only the first word of the header or title is capitalized:

El autor de la novela Cien años de soledad *es Gabriel García Márquez.*

The author of the novel *A Hundred Years of Solitude* is Gabriel García Márquez.

El primer capítulo de este libro se llama "Bienvenidos al mundo del idioma castellano".

The first chapter of this book is called "Welcome to the World of Spanish."

¿Has visto la película Tráfico?

Have you seen the movie *Traffic?*

That's All for Spanish

This pretty much takes care of capitalization in Spanish. Although we have additional capitalization rules in English, none of them apply in Spanish.

Days of the Week

In Spanish, the days of the week are written in lowercase letters: *lunes, martes, miércoles, jueves, viernes, sábado, domingo* (Monday, Tuesday, and so on).

Months of the Year

The same is true of the twelve months of the year: *enero, febrero, marzo, abril, mayo, junio, julio, agosto, septiembre, octubre, noviembre, diciembre* (January, February, and so on).

FACT

In Spanish, title abbreviations like *Sr.* (Mr.) and *Dr.* (Dr.) are capitalized, but written out titles are not: *señor García, doctor Sánchez, doctora Flores.* Also note that for the feminine title *doctora,* the abbreviation is *Dra.*

Languages and Nationality

It is unnecessary to capitalize languages and nationalities:

Yo soy rusa. Hablo ruso, inglés y castellano.

I am Russian. I speak Russian, English, and Spanish.

¿Se habla francés en Canadá?

Is French spoken in Canada?

Religious Denominations

Finally, don't worry about capitalizing names of religions:

Soy judía; mi religión es judaísmo.

I am Jewish; my religion is Judaism.

La religión más común entre los latinos es el catolicismo.

The most common religion among Latinos is Catholicism.

The Rules of Punctuation

As with capitalization, the general rules of punctuation in Spanish are not very different from the rules in English. The punctuation signs in use are pretty much the same:

- *El punto* (period) is used to mark the end of the sentence.
- *La coma* (comma) has a variety of uses, such as separating a series of like terms, except when the comma precedes the conjunctions *y*, *e*, *o*, and *u*
- *Dos puntos* (colon) is used to introduce a point or a series of terms.
- *Punto y coma* (semicolon) is used to separate independent clauses.
- *El guión* (dash, hyphen) has the same applications in English and in Spanish, but it has an additional use in Spanish.
- *Los signos de interrogación* (question marks) are used to indicate questions. The difference, as you might remember from Chapter 16, is that you need two question marks to enclose the question.
- *Los signos de exclamación* (exclamation marks) are used to indicate exclamations. You need two exclamation marks to enclose the exclamation.
- *Comillas* (quotation marks) are used in Spanish only in the case of highlighting a word, phrase, or a quote; they're not used to indicate dialogue.

The major difference between English and Spanish pronunciation is punctuating words of dialogue. Instead of quotation marks, a dash is used in Spanish to indicate the start of dialogue. Furthermore, there's no rule that each speaker's words are separated by a hard return. Take a look at the following example:

—Estoy tan cansado— dijo Ramón. —Vamos a descansar por un rato— respondió Elena.

"I am so tired," said Ramon.

"Let's rest a while," responded Elena.

Another difference is that commas and periods are placed outside of quotation marks, unless these punctuation marks are a part of the original quote: . . . *"ejemplo"*, . . . *"ejemplo"*.

The final difference is the use of the comma and period in decimals and numerals with more than three digits. In Spanish, the usage is inverted so that decimal points are separated with a comma and numerals with more than three digits are separated by periods:

Two thousand = 2.000

Two and a quarter = 2,25

When in Doubt—Look It Up

If you plan to write on your PC or Mac, there's good news–you can probably switch your language option to Spanish and your word processing program may even provide you with a spell checker and a grammar checker. Even if it's not already installed on your computer, you can probably download good software online.

The extra effort is definitely worth it. The software can help you catch mistakes so that next time you'll do it right the first time. However, don't forget that no program is perfect–it's meant to be a good resource, but you shouldn't accept all the corrections without question. As in English, you still have to make decisions about what is right and what is wrong. A spell checker will not catch you misusing a Spanish word–it can only catch misspellings. Similarly, a grammar checker may point out a commonly misused grammatical construction that you used correctly. Trust yourself to know which mistakes are really mistakes.

ESSENTIAL

A quick glance at the dictionary isn't always enough. Often a word will have several different translations and you need to choose the appropriate one based on the context. For example, if you want to describe hair as brown, you can't say *el cabello café*. *Café* does mean "brown," but is not used to describe hair color. *Marrón* (dark brown) or *castaño* (chestnut-colored) are better choices.

And when you are in doubt, double-check yourself. In addition to this book, there are many other resources you can rely on. If you feel uncomfortable with verb conjugations, invest in *The Everything® Spanish Verb Book*. And make sure you have a good Spanish to English/English to Spanish dictionary with detailed entries, like *The Oxford Spanish Dictionary* or the *Larousse Standard Dictionary: Spanish-English/English-Spanish*.

You can also take advantage of online resources. Wordreference.com provides online dictionaries for Spanish, English, and a host of other languages. Verb conjugation help is also available online, but be sure that you're using a reputable Web site that is not full of mistakes and misinformation.

Accent Marks, Ñ, and Other Symbols

If you can switch to Spanish in your word processing software, it may auto-correct you when you type by adding the right Spanish symbols as appropriate—the accent marks over vowels, the tilde (that squiggly mark over the soft "n"), and even upside-down question marks and exclamation marks (¿ and ¡). Test it out and see if it works. For questions and exclamations, try starting with a regular question mark or exclamation mark—the symbol should flip upside-down automatically.

If you don't have Spanish as a language option, or if your paper is mostly in English but requires the use of Spanish passages, you'll need to learn the shortcuts for inserting the right symbols and accents as you type.

On a PC

One way to insert accent marks, ñ, ¿, and ¡ is by using the Symbol menu usually found on the toolbar under the Tools category. Scroll down to find the right symbol, click on it, and press Insert. You'll see it appear in the document.

Another option is to use a series of shortcut key strokes. To add an accent mark, first press down and release two keys: **Control** + **'** (apostrophe). Then type in the vowel that you wish to accent: a, e, i, o, or u. To key in ñ, press down **Control** + ~ (this is actually three keys, since ~ is a combination of **Shift** + \`). Release and type in "n." If á, é, í, ó, ú, or ñ are capital letters, use Shift when you type a, e, i, o, u, or n.

To add an upside-down question mark, use the following key strokes: **Shift** + **Control** + **Alt** + **?** If you need an upside-down exclamation mark, type in **Shift** + **Control** + **Alt** + **!** And there's more good news—if you don't like these shortcuts, you may be able to make your own. Go back to that Symbol window and poke around.

On a Mac

If you're using the Mac version of Microsoft Word, the Symbol menu is pretty much identical—just look under Tools. But if you'd like to use the shortcut key strokes, they're slightly different.

To add an accent mark to a vowel, hold down **Option** + **e;** release, then type in the vowel that needs the accent—a, e, i, o, or u. Again, if the accented vowel is a capital letter, add the **Shift** key to the second step. To insert "ñ," simply type in **Option + n** (or **Option + Shift + n** to get Ñ).

And adding ¿ and ¡ is even easier. To get the upside-down question mark, type in **Option + ?** For the upside-down exclamation mark, use **Option + 1.**

ESSENTIAL

If you don't have access to Microsoft Word or a similar software program and you can't figure out how to add the accent marks and other symbols, print out your work and add the symbols in with a black pen—and don't forget to leave an extra space for the upside-down question marks and exclamation marks.

Composing a Letter

Overall, writing in Spanish isn't very different. You can use the same formats you've always relied on when composing poems, short stories, essays, and other forms of writing. None of these forms are very rigid in their structure and there aren't really any conventions you need to be aware of.

The one exception to this rule is letter-writing. Learning how to compose formal and informal letters will come in handy if you'd like to have a Spanish-speaking pen-pal, if you're planning to study or work abroad, or if your business has international branches and you need to communicate with them for professional reasons.

Formal Letters

Begin your letter by writing the place (where you are) and date in the top right hand corner. You can use the following format:

Nueva York, 2 de enero de 2005

Buenos Aires, 20 de marzo de 2006

Springfield, Ohio, 15 de septiembre de 2007

Next, include the "dear –" line. If you know whom you're writing to, you can simply use *Señor* (or *Señora/Señores/Señoras*); another option is to add *estimado* (esteemed):

Estimado Señor

Estimada Señora

Estimados Señores

Estimadas Señoras

If the addressee is unknown, you can write *A quien corresponda* (to whom it may concern). The biggest difference here is that there's no punctuation (comma or colon) at the end of this line.

Insert an extra space and continue with the body of the letter. There are no rules here. Write down what needs to be communicated and don't forget to be polite and use the *usted/ustedes* form of address.

To close the letter, choose any of the following formal closings:

Atentamente	Sincerely
Atentos saludos de	Sincere greetings from
Un cordial saludo	A cordial greeting

Again, there's no punctuation following the closing. Simply sign your name underneath. If you need to add a post scriptum (P.S.) line, it should be labeled P.D. *(post data).*

Informal Letters

If your letter is informal, there are a few things you would do differently. One common way of addressing your reader or readers is with the adjective *querido* (dear):

Querida Ana	Dear Ana
Querido hermano	Dear brother
Queridos amigos	Dear friends

In closing, appropriate sign-offs include the following:

Un abrazo de	With a hug
Un cariñoso saludo	An affectionate greeting
Tu amiga	Your friend

CHAPTER 19

Spanish in Everyday Life

CONGRATULATIONS! You've made it through the rules, exceptions, and general guidelines that make up Spanish grammar. The last chapter in this book is your opportunity to apply what you've learned to specific situations and to review basic vocabulary.

Physical Characteristics

¿Cómo te ves? What do you look like? To answer, you can use the verb *ser* (to be) and *tener* (to have), plus a series of adjectives that describe your stature, hair and eye color, and so on. For example:

Yo soy alto y delgado. Tengo el pelo corto de color castaño y los ojos azules.

I am tall and thin. I have chestnut-colored hair and blue eyes.

Here's some useful vocabulary for describing yourself and others.

Estatura y tamaño (Height and Size)	
alto	tall
bajo	short
mediano	medium
gordo, corpulento	fat
delgado, flaco	thin

El cabello **(Hair)**	
corto	short
largo	long
liso	straight
rizado	curly
rubio	blond
pelirrojo	red
castaño	chestnut-colored
moreno	brown, dark brown
negro	black
canoso	gray

Los ojos **(Eyes)**	
azul	blue
pardo, marrón	brown
negro	black
verde	green
color de avellana	hazel
claro	light
oscuro	dark

Other Adjectives	
joven	young
viejo	old
bonito	pretty
bello	beautiful
guapo	cute
feo	ugly
interesante	interesting
simpático	nice

Family Relations

La familia (the family) plays an important part in the lives of the people living around the Spanish world. To get all the relationships straight, here's some relevant vocabulary:

Los parientes (Relatives)	
madre	mother
padre	father
padres	parents
marido, esposo	husband
esposa, mujer	wife
hijo, hija	son, daughter
hermano, hermana	brother, sister
gemelo, mellizo	twin
abuelo, abuela	grandfather, grandmother
nieto, nieta	grandson, granddaughter
tío, tía	uncle, aunt
sobrino, sobrina	nephew, niece
primo	cousin

suegro, suegra	father-in-law, mother-in-law
yerno	son-in-law
nuera	daughter-in-law
padrino	godfather
madrina	godmother
de acogida	foster

ESSENTIAL

In parts of Latin America, particularly the Spanish-speaking Caribbean and Central America, you might hear a man address a woman as *mami* and a woman address a man as *papi*. This is limited to very informal situations—you may want to avoid using these words unless you're sure they're appropriate.

You can practice the vocabulary by reviewing your family tree. For example:

Me llamo Jorge. Soy ingeniero. Mis padres son Juan y Renata. Mi padre es médico; mi madre es enfermera. Yo estoy casado con María. Ella es una actriz de teatro. Mi esposa y yo tenemos dos hijos: Elena y Daniel. Elena es estudiante en la escuela secundaria. Daniel asiste a la universidad. También tengo una hermana, Marta. Ella vive en Colombia. Trabaja en un banco. Marta tiene un hijo, Cristóbal. A Elena y Daniel les gusta visitar a su tía y a sus primos en Colombia.

How much were you able to understand? To help you make sense of it, here's the translation:

My name is Jorge. I'm an engineer. My parents are Juan and Renata. My father is a doctor; my mother is a nurse. I am married to María. She is a theater actress. My wife and I have two kids: Elena and Daniel. Elena is a high school student. Daniel goes to college. I also have a sister, Marta. She lives in Colombia. She works at a bank. Marta has a son, Cristóbal. Elena and Daniel like to visit their aunt and cousins in Colombia.

Now, how about trying to describe your own family? What are they like?

Back to School

Whether you're in high school, college, or back in school to brush up on your Spanish, you can really impress your instructor if you are comfortable with some classroom vocabulary. You probably know a lot of these terms–review the ones you do know and commit to memory the vocabulary you haven't encountered before.

En la clase **(In the Classroom)**	
estudiante	student
profesor, profesora	high school teacher
maestro	elementary school teacher
catedrático	professor
pluma, bolígrafo	pen
lápiz	pencil
goma de borrar	pencil eraser
papel	paper
cuaderno	notebook
libro	book
carpeta	folder

mochila	backpack
pizarra	board
tiza	chalk
borrador	board eraser
reloj	clock, watch
silla	chair
escritorio	desk
cartel	poster
cesta	wastebasket

If your Spanish classes are conducted in Spanish, it'll help to know some basic phrases as well. Here are a few to get you started:

¿Cómo se dice grades *en castellano?*
How do you say "grades" in Spanish?

Señor Blanco, ¿puede usted repetir su pregunta, por favor?
Mr. White, can you please repeat your question?

¿Cuándo tendremos el examen final?
When are we having the final exam?

No entiendo cómo conjugar el verbo "ser". Explíquemelo, por favor.
I don't know how to conjugate the verb *ser.* Please explain it to me.

¿Podemos usar el diccionario durante la prueba?
Can we use the dictionary during the quiz?

¿Puedo ir al baño, por favor?

May I please go to the bathroom?

Eating Out

To practice your Spanish, try eating out at local restaurants that serve Spanish, Caribbean, or Mexican fare. Lots of students of Spanish enjoy going out to a Spanish tapas bar. And many others have forsworn the local Tex-Mex hangout in favor of authentic Mexican restaurants that serve dishes like *mole, chiles rellenos,* and *sopa de frijoles negros* (meat in chile sauce, stuffed peppers, and black bean soup).

QUESTION?

What are tapas?

Tapas are small appetizer-sized dishes like *aceitunas* (olives) or *jamón serrano* (Spanish cured ham) eaten instead of a main course. Tapas originated in southern Spain as bar snacks. Some say *tapa* comes from the word "to cover" because bartenders used to cover a glass with a little plate to keep flies away and eventually started adding a bit of food to the plate. Others say it comes from the phrase *tapar el apetito* (put a lid on the appetite).

When you're out at a local burrito joint—or even if you're at the only Peruvian restaurant in town—you can try ordering in Spanish and sticking to the Spanish side of the menu, but you can always fall back on English if necessary. But if you travel abroad, you may not have that luxury. Here are some common dishes you may encounter on the menu in Spain, Mexico, Puerto Rico, or anywhere else in the Spanish-speaking world.

On the Menu	
carta, menú	menu
antojito	appetizer
ensalada	salad
sopa	soup
caldo	broth
pescado	fish
mariscos	seafood
ave	poultry
carne	meat
salsa	sauce
legumbres	vegetables or legume
vegetales	green vegetables
pan	bread
postre	dessert
bebida	drink

Common Menu Items	
ceviche	fish or seafood cured in lemon juice
empanada	savory stuffed pastry, usually with meat
chuleta	(pork) chop
bistec	(beef) steak
hígado	liver
salchicha	pork sausage
salpicón	cold non-vegetable salad (usually with seafood)
chorizo	pork sausage

lomo de cerdo	pork loin
tocino	salted pork
pozole	hominy stew
tortilla española	Spanish potato omelette
croqueta	croquette
mofongo	mashed plantains, often with seafood
al ajillo	in garlic sauce
al horno	baked
arroz con frijoles	rice and beans
paella	a saffron rice dish, usually prepared with seafood
arepa	corn pancake
tamales	corn patties, usually with minced meat
yucca	a root vegetable similar to a potato
tostones	savory fried plantains
maduros	sweet (ripe) fried plantains
arroz con leche	rice pudding
batido	milk shake
helado	ice cream
flan	custard
buñuelo	fritter
sangría	a mix of wine and fruit juices
café	coffee
agua	water
jugo	juice

Even if you can't figure out the name of the dish, you might get the general idea of the dish from the list of ingredients. Here is some vocabulary to help you along.

Meat, Poultry, and Fish	
carne de cerdo	pork
carne de res	beef
jamón	ham
cordero	lamb
ternera	veal
chivo	goat
pollo	chicken
pato	duck
pavo	turkey
bacalao	cod
atún	tuna
langosta	lobster
gamba	large shrimp
camarón	shrimp
calamar	squid, calamari
mejillón	mussel

Fruits and Vegetables	
cebolla	onion
ajo	garlic
tomate	tomato
lechuga	lettuce
aguacate	avocado
papas	potatoes
maíz	corn
champiñón	mushroom
espinaca	spinach

coliflor	cauliflower
berenjena	eggplant
aceituna	olive
piña	pineapple
naranja	orange
manzana	apple
pomelo	grapefruit
uva	grape
fresa	strawberry
frambuesa	raspberry

Other Ingredients	
arroz	rice
lenteja	lentil
huevo	egg
aceite	oil
vinagre	vinegar
mantequilla	butter
queso	cheese
leche	milk
crema	cream
azúcar	sugar
sal	salt
pimienta	pepper

Looking for a Job

Traveling is good for your language skills, but an even better way to start speaking like the locals is to get a job in a Spanish-speaking country. If you're in school and have the opportunity to spend a semester abroad, you can find an internship that will help you improve your professional skills and your foreign language. And if you're out in the real world, there are many programs available to those interested in spending some time abroad. You can do volunteer work, teach English, or maybe even get a job in your career field.

***Buscando empleo* (Looking for a Job)**	
empleo	job
curriculum profesional	resume
carta de acompañamiento	cover letter
habilidad	ability, skill
anuncio de trabajo	help-wanted ad
entrevista	interview
salario	salary, wages
jefe	boss

Putting Together a Resume

If you're serious about your job search, it'll help to have a good resume. If you've already got one in English, you'll have to change a few things, but the idea is the same. In your resume, include your name and address, date of birth, education, work experience, and skills.

Sample Resume

Datos personales
Nombre y apellido: Janet Morton
Lugar y fecha de nacimiento: San Francisco, 5 de abril de 1979
Dirección: 3 calle Main, #15, Boston, MA 01905
Teléfono: 617-555-1234

Formación
El Colegio San Bernardo, 1993-1997, calificación de notable.

Licenciado en Educación Bilingüe, UCLA, 1997-2001.

Idiomas
Castellano: leído, hablado, escrito y traducido (nivel alto).
Italiano: leído y hablado (nivel medio).

Informática
Microsoft Office, HTML

Experiencia profesional
Profesora del programa Inglés Como Segundo Idioma, escuela de Boston. Septiembre de 2001-mayo de 2003.

Directora del programa Inglés Como Segundo Idioma, escuela de Boston. Junio de 2003-el día presente.

As you can see, the first section should cover *datos personales* (personal information). In the United States, it is inappropriate for the employer to ask about your age, let alone expect you to list it on your resume. In Spain and in some parts of Latin America, however, indicating the *fecha de nacimiento* (date of birth)–as well as *lugar de nacimiento* (place of birth)–is still appropriate.

The next section is *formación* or education. List all education, from your high school *(el colegio)* to your degrees. Next are *idiomas* (languages) and *informática* (computer skills). The last part of your resume should be a list of work experiences, starting with the earliest. In a more detailed resume, you can also include a description of each job.

Surfing the Web

Even if going abroad is not an option—or at least not an option as of yet, don't despair. You've got the whole world at your fingertips. All you need is your computer and a way to log on to the World Wide Web, and you can visit faraway places where people speak Spanish and join in their conversations. Here's some vocabulary to help get you started.

La Web: Vocabulario	
punto	. (dot)
barra	/ (slash)
herramienta	tool
Red	network
contraseña	password
correo electrónico	e-mail
impresora	printer
en línea	online
fuera de línea	offline
botón	key
página de la Web	Web page
página principal	home page
buscar	search
sitio	site

APPENDIX A

Verb Tables

Hablar (to speak)/Regular –AR verb		
	Present	**Subjunctive**
yo	hablo	hable
tú	hablas	hables
él	habla	hable
nosotros	hablamos	hablemos
vosotros	habláis	habléis
ellos	hablan	hablen
	Preterite	**Imperfect**
yo	hablé	hablaba
tú	hablaste	hablabas
él	habló	hablaba
nosotros	hablamos	hablábamos
vosotros	hablasteis	hablabais
ellos	hablaron	hablaban
	Future	**Conditional**
yo	hablaré	hablaría
tú	hablarás	hablarías
él	hablará	hablaría
nosotros	hablaremos	hablaríamos
vosotros	hablaréis	hablaríais
ellos	hablarán	hablarían
Imperfect Subjunctive	**Form 1**	**Form 2**
yo	hablara	hablase
tú	hablaras	hablases
él	hablara	hablase
nosotros	habláramos	hablásemos
vosotros	hablarais	hablaseis
ellos	hablaran	hablasen
	Command	**Present Participle**
(tú)	habla	hablando
	no hables	
(Ud.)	hable	
(nosotros)	hablemos	**Past Participle**
(vosotros)	hablad	hablado
	no habléis	
(Uds.)	hablen	

Vender (to sell) / Regular –ER verb

	Present	**Subjunctive**
yo	vendo	venda
tú	vendes	vendas
él	vende	venda
nosotros	vendemos	vendamos
vosotros	vendéis	vendáis
ellos	venden	vendan
	Preterite	**Imperfect**
yo	vendí	vendía
tú	vendiste	vendías
él	vendió	vendía
nosotros	vendimos	vendíamos
vosotros	vendisteis	vendíais
ellos	vendieron	vendían
	Future	**Conditional**
yo	venderé	vendería
tú	venderás	venderías
él	venderá	vendería
nosotros	venderemos	venderíamos
vosotros	venderéis	venderíais
ellos	venderán	venderían
Imperfect Subjunctive	**Form 1**	**Form 2**
yo	vendiera	vendiese
tú	vendieras	vendieses
él	vendiera	vendiese
nosotros	vendiéramos	vendiésemos
vosotros	vendierais	vendieseis
ellos	vendieran	vendiesen
	Command	**Present Participle**
(tú)	vende	vendiendo
	no vendas	
(Ud.)	venda	
(nosotros)	vendamos	**Past Participle**
(vosotros)	vended	vendido
	no vendáis	
(Uds.)	vendan	

Vivir (to live) / Regular –IR verb

	Present	Subjunctive
yo	vivo	viva
tú	vives	vivas
él	vive	viva
nosotros	vivimos	vivamos
vosotros	vivís	viváis
ellos	viven	vivan
	Preterite	**Imperfect**
yo	viví	vivía
tú	viviste	vivías
él	vivió	vivía
nosotros	vivimos	vivíamos
vosotros	vivisteis	vivíais
ellos	vivieron	vivían
	Future	**Conditional**
yo	viviré	viviría
tú	vivirás	vivirías
él	vivirá	viviría
nosotros	viviremos	viviríamos
vosotros	viviréis	viviríais
ellos	vivirán	vivirían
Imperfect Subjunctive	**Form 1**	**Form 2**
yo	viviera	viviese
tú	vivieras	vivieses
él	viviera	viviese
nosotros	viviéramos	viviésemos
vosotros	vivierais	vivieseis
ellos	vivieran	viviesen
	Command	**Present Participle**
(tú)	vive	viviendo
	no vivas	
(Ud.)	viva	
(nosotros)	vivamos	**Past Participle**
(vosotros)	vivid	vivido
	no viváis	
(Uds.)	vivan	

Cerrar (to close) / Stem-changing (E > IE) –AR verb

	Present	**Subjunctive**
yo	cierro	cierre
tú	cierras	cierres
él	cierra	cierre
nosotros	cerramos	cerremos
vosotros	cerráis	cerréis
ellos	cierran	cierren
	Preterite	**Imperfect**
yo	cerré	cerraba
tú	cerraste	cerrabas
él	cerró	cerraba
nosotros	cerramos	cerrábamos
vosotros	cerrasteis	cerrabais
ellos	cerraron	cerraban
	Future	**Conditional**
yo	cerraré	cerraría
tú	cerrarás	cerrarías
él	cerrará	cerraría
nosotros	cerraremos	cerraríamos
vosotros	cerraréis	cerraríais
ellos	cerrarán	cerrarían
Imperfect Subjunctive	**Form 1**	**Form 2**
yo	cerrara	cerrase
tú	cerraras	cerrases
él	cerrara	cerrase
nosotros	cerráramos	cerrásemos
vosotros	cerrarais	cerraseis
ellos	cerraran	cerrasen
	Command	**Present Participle**
(tú)	cierra	cerrando
	no cierres	
(Ud.)	cierre	
(nosotros)	cerremos	**Past Participle**
(vosotros)	cerrad	cerrado
	no cerréis	
(Uds.)	cierren	

Conocer (to know) / Spelling-change (C > ZC) –ER verb

	Present	Subjunctive
yo	conozco	conozca
tú	conoces	conozcas
él	conoce	conozca
nosotros	conocemos	conozcamos
vosotros	conocéis	conozcáis
ellos	conocen	conozcan
	Preterite	**Imperfect**
yo	conocí	conocía
tú	conociste	conocías
él	conoció	conocía
nosotros	conocimos	conocíamos
vosotros	conocisteis	conocíais
ellos	conocieron	conocían
	Future	**Conditional**
yo	conoceré	conocería
tú	conocerás	conocerías
él	conocerá	conocería
nosotros	conoceremos	conoceríamos
vosotros	conoceréis	conoceríais
ellos	conocerán	conocerían
Imperfect Subjunctive	**Form 1**	**Form 2**
yo	conociera	conociese
tú	conocieras	conocieses
él	conociera	conociese
nosotros	conociéramos	conociésemos
vosotros	conocierais	conocieseis
ellos	conocieran	conociesen
	Command	**Present Participle**
(tú)	conoce	conociendo
	no conozcas	
(Ud.)	conozca	
(nosotros)	conozcamos	**Past Participle**
(vosotros)	conoced	conocido
	no conozcáis	
(Uds.)	conozcan	

Dar (to give) / Iregular –AR verb

	Present	Subjunctive
yo	doy	dé
tú	das	des
él	da	dé
nosotros	damos	demos
vosotros	dais	deis
ellos	dan	den
	Preterite	**Imperfect**
yo	di	daba
tú	diste	dabas
él	dio	daba
nosotros	dimos	dábamos
vosotros	disteis	dabais
ellos	dieron	daban
	Future	**Conditional**
yo	daré	daría
tú	darás	darías
él	dará	daría
nosotros	daremos	daríamos
vosotros	daréis	daríais
ellos	darán	darían
Imperfect Subjunctive	**Form 1**	**Form 2**
yo	diera	diese
tú	dieras	dieses
él	diera	diese
nosotros	diéramos	diésemos
vosotros	dierais	dieseis
ellos	dieran	diesen
	Command	**Present Participle**
(tú)	da	dando
	no des	
(Ud.)	dé	
(nosotros)	demos	**Past Participle**
(vosotros)	dad	dado
	no deis	
(Uds.)	den	

Dormir (to sleep) / Stem-changing (O > UE) –IR verb

	Present	Subjunctive
yo	duermo	duerma
tú	duermes	duermas
él	duerme	duerma
nosotros	dormimos	durmamos
vosotros	dormís	durmáis
ellos	duermen	duerman
	Preterite	**Imperfect**
yo	dormí	dormía
tú	dormiste	dormías
él	durmió	dormía
nosotros	dormimos	dormíamos
vosotros	dormisteis	dormíais
ellos	durmieron	dormían
	Future	**Conditional**
yo	dormiré	dormiría
tú	dormirás	dormirías
él	dormirá	dormiría
nosotros	dormiremos	dormiríamos
vosotros	dormiréis	dormiríais
ellos	dormirán	dormirían
Imperfect Subjunctive	**Form 1**	**Form 2**
yo	durmiera	durmiese
tú	durmieras	durmieses
él	durmiera	durmiese
nosotros	durmiéramos	durmiésemos
vosotros	durmierais	durmieseis
ellos	durmieran	durmiesen
	Command	**Present Participle**
(tú)	duerme	durmiendo
	no duermas	
(Ud.)	duerma	
(nosotros)	durmamos	**Past Participle**
(vosotros)	dormid	dormido
	no durmáis	
(Uds.)	duerman	

Estar (to be) / Irregular –AR verb

	Present	Subjunctive
yo	estoy	esté
tú	estás	estés
él	está	esté
nosotros	estamos	estemos
vosotros	estáis	estéis
ellos	están	estén
	Preterite	**Imperfect**
yo	estuve	estaba
tú	estuviste	estabas
él	estuvo	estaba
nosotros	estuvimos	estábamos
vosotros	estuvisteis	estabais
ellos	estuvieron	estaban
	Future	**Conditional**
yo	estaré	estaría
tú	estarás	estarías
él	estará	estaría
nosotros	estaremos	estaríamos
vosotros	estaréis	estaríais
ellos	estarán	estarían
Imperfect Subjunctive	**Form 1**	**Form 2**
yo	estuviera	estuviese
tú	estuvieras	estuvieses
él	estuviera	estuviese
nosotros	estuviéramos	estuviésemos
vosotros	estuvierais	estuvieseis
ellos	estuvieran	estuviesen
	Command	**Present Participle**
(tú)	está	estando
	no estés	
(Ud.)	esté	
(nosotros)	estemos	**Past Participle**
(vosotros)	estad	estado
	no estéis	
(Uds.)	estén	

Hacer (to do, to make) / Irregular –ER verb

	Present	Subjunctive
yo	hago	haga
tú	haces	hagas
él	hace	haga
nosotros	hacemos	hagamos
vosotros	hacéis	hagáis
ellos	hacen	hagan
	Preterite	**Imperfect**
yo	hice	hacía
tú	hiciste	hacías
él	hizo	hacía
nosotros	hicimos	hacíamos
vosotros	hicisteis	hacíais
ellos	hicieron	hacían
	Future	**Conditional**
yo	haré	haría
tú	harás	harías
él	hará	haría
nosotros	haremos	haríamos
vosotros	haréis	haríais
ellos	harán	harían
Imperfect Subjunctive	**Form 1**	**Form 2**
yo	hiciera	hiciese
tú	hicieras	hicieses
él	hiciera	hiciese
nosotros	hiciéramos	hiciésemos
vosotros	hicierais	hicieseis
ellos	hicieran	hiciesen
	Command	**Present Participle**
(tú)	haz	haciendo
	no hagas	
(Ud.)	haga	
(nosotros)	hagamos	**Past Participle**
(vosotros)	haced	hecho
	no hagáis	
(Uds.)	hagan	

Ir (to go) / Irregular –IR verb

	Present	Subjunctive
yo	voy	vaya
tú	vas	vayas
él	va	vaya
nosotros	vamos	vayamos
vosotros	vais	vayáis
ellos	van	vayan
	Preterite	**Imperfect**
yo	fui	iba
tú	fuiste	ibas
él	fue	iba
nosotros	fuimos	íbamos
vosotros	fuisteis	ibais
ellos	fueron	iban
	Future	**Conditional**
yo	iré	iría
tú	irás	irías
él	irá	iría
nosotros	iremos	iríamos
vosotros	iréis	iríais
ellos	irán	irían
Imperfect Subjunctive	**Form 1**	**Form 2**
yo	fuera	fuese
tú	fueras	fueses
él	fuera	fuese
nosotros	fuéramos	fuésemos
vosotros	fuerais	fueseis
ellos	fueran	fuesen
	Command	**Present Participle**
(tú)	ve	yendo
	no vayas	
(Ud.)	vaya	
(nosotros)	vamos	**Past Participle**
	no vayamos	ido
(vosotros)	id	
	no vayáis	
(Uds.)	vayan	

Saber (to know) / Irregular –ER verb

	Present	Subjunctive
yo	sé	sepa
tú	sabes	sepas
él	sabe	sepa
nosotros	sabemos	sepamos
vosotros	sabéis	sepáis
ellos	saben	sepan
	Preterite	**Imperfect**
yo	supe	sabía
tú	supiste	sabías
él	supo	sabía
nosotros	supimos	sabíamos
vosotros	supisteis	sabíais
ellos	supieron	sabían
	Future	**Conditional**
yo	sabré	sabría
tú	sabrás	sabrías
él	sabrá	sabría
nosotros	sabremos	sabríamos
vosotros	sabréis	sabríais
ellos	sabrán	sabrían
Imperfect Subjunctive	**Form 1**	**Form 2**
yo	supiera	supiese
tú	supieras	supieses
él	supiera	supiese
nosotros	supiéramos	supiésemos
vosotros	supierais	supieseis
ellos	supieran	supiesen
	Command	**Present Participle**
(tú)	sabe	sabiendo
	no sepas	
(Ud.)	sepa	
(nosotros)	sepamos	**Past Participle**
(vosotros)	sabed	sabido
	no sepáis	
(Uds.)	sepan	

Ser (to be) / Irregular –ER verb		
	Present	**Subjunctive**
yo	soy	sea
tú	eres	seas
él	es	sea
nosotros	somos	seamos
vosotros	sois	seáis
ellos	son	sean
	Preterite	**Imperfect**
yo	fui	era
tú	fuiste	eras
él	fue	era
nosotros	fuimos	éramos
vosotros	fuisteis	erais
ellos	fueron	eran
	Future	**Conditional**
yo	seré	sería
tú	serás	serías
él	será	sería
nosotros	seremos	seríamos
vosotros	seréis	seríais
ellos	serán	serían
Imperfect Subjunctive	**Form 1**	**Form 2**
yo	fuera	fuese
tú	fueras	fueses
él	fuera	fuese
nosotros	fuéramos	fuésemos
vosotros	fuerais	fueseis
ellos	fueran	fuesen
	Command	**Present Participle**
(tú)	sé	siendo
	no seas	
(Ud.)	sea	
(nosotros)	seamos	**Past Participle**
(vosotros)	sed	sido
	no seáis	
(Uds.)	sean	

Tener (to have) / Irregular –ER verb

	Present	Subjunctive
yo	tengo	tenga
tú	tienes	tengas
él	tiene	tenga
nosotros	tenemos	tengamos
vosotros	tenéis	tengáis
ellos	tienen	tengan
	Preterite	**Imperfect**
yo	tuve	tenía
tú	tuviste	tenías
él	tuvo	tenía
nosotros	tuvimos	teníamos
vosotros	tuvisteis	teníais
ellos	tuvieron	tenían
	Future	**Conditional**
yo	tendré	tendría
tú	tendrás	tendrías
él	tendrá	tendría
nosotros	tendremos	tendríamos
vosotros	tendréis	tendríais
ellos	tendrán	tendrían
Imperfect Subjunctive	**Form 1**	**Form 2**
yo	tuviera	tuviese
tú	tuvieras	tuvieses
él	tuviera	tuviese
nosotros	tuviéramos	tuviésemos
vosotros	tuvierais	tuvieseis
ellos	tuvieran	tuviesen
	Command	**Present Participle**
(tú)	ten	teniendo
	no tengas	
(Ud.)	tenga	
(nosotros)	tengamos	**Past Participle**
(vosotros)	tened	tenido
	no tengáis	
(Uds.)	tengan	

APPENDIX B

English to Spanish Glossary

A

a little poco
a lot mucho
a while un rato
ability la habilidad
abroad el extranjero
academic escolástico
to achieve conseguir
accomplice el consorte
according to según
accuser el acusador
accusing acusador
across from enfrente a, frente a
to achieve conseguir
to act actuar
actress la actriz
to actualize realizar
actually la verdad es que
address la dirección
to address with *tú* tutearse
adjective el adjetivo
adverb el adverbio
to advise aconsejar
affectionate cariñoso
to afflict afligir
after después de
afternoon la tarde
again otra vez
against the grain contrapelo
against contra
Algeria Argelia
Algerian argelino
all todo
almost casi
alone solo
already ya
although aunque
always siempre
American estadounidense
amusing gracioso
anarchy la anarquía
ancient antiguo
to announce anunciar
to annoy molestar, fastidiar
annoying fastidioso
another otro
answer la respuesta, la solución
to answer contestar, responder
antipathy la antipatía
antiperspirant el antisudoral
apartment el apartamento
to appear aparecer
appetite el apetito
appetizer el antojito
applause el aplauso
apple la manzana
apprenticeship el aprendizaje
to approach acercarse
April abril
Argentinean argentino
around alrededor
around here acá
to arrange arreglar
to arrive llegar
as como
as . . . as tan . . . como
as much/many cuanto
as soon as en cuanto
to ask pedir
to ask (a question) preguntar
at least lo menos
at present actualmente
atheism el ateísmo
attempt el intento
to attend asistir
attention la atención
attentive atento
attitude la actitud
to attribute atribuir
August agosto
aunt la tía
Australian australiano
Austrian austríaco
author el autor
authorization la autorización
autobiography la autobiografía
avarice la avaricia
average medio
avocado el aguacate
to award otorgar

B

baby el bebé
back cover la contracubierta
backpack la mochila
bad mal(o)
baked al horno
bakery la panadería
bank el banco
banker el bancario
to bathe bañar
to be ser
to be (located) estar
to be able to poder
to be bored aburrirse
to be born nacer
to be happy alegrarse
to be important importar(le)
to be quiet callarse
to be surprised sorprenderse
to be well behaved comportarse bien
to be worth valer
beach la playa
beans los frijoles
beautiful bello
because porque
to become hacerse
bed la cama
bedroom el dormitorio
bee la abeja

beef	la carne de res
before	antes
beforehand	antemano
to beg	rogar
to begin (to)	empezar (a), comenzar (a)
behind	detrás
Belgian	belga
Belgium	Bélgica
to believe	creer
bell tower	el campanario
to belong	pertenecer
bench	el banco
best	mejor
between	entre
bill	la cuenta
billion	los mil millones
birth	el nacimiento
birthday	el cumpleaños
black	negro
to blink	parpadear
blond	rubio
blue	azul
board	la pizarra
boat	el bote
body	el cuerpo
Bolivian	boliviano
book	el libro
bookshelf	el estante
bookstore	la librería
to bore	aburrir
bored, boring	aburrido
boss	el jefe, la jefa
both	ambos, ambas
to bother	molestar
to bother oneself	lastimarse
box	la caja
boy	el chico, el niño
boyfriend	el novio
Brazil	el Brasil
Brazilian	brasileño
bread	el pan
to break	romper(se)
to break (a bone)	quebrarse
to break (something)	quebrar
breakfast	el desayuno
bright	claro
to bring	traer
to bring to a halt	detener
brother	el hermano
brotherhood	la hermandad
brown	café, marrón
to brush (teeth, hair)	cepillar(se)
building	el edificio
to burn	quemar
bus	el autobús
but	pero, mas
but (following a neg. statement)	sino
butter	la mantequilla
to buy	comprar
by	por

C

cab driver	el/la taxista
cada	cada
cake	la torta
calamari	los calamares
to call	llamar
calmness	la quietud
camp	el campamento
Canada	el Canadá
Canadian	canadiense
candle	la vela
candy, sweet	el dulce
caprice	el capricho
car	el coche
care	el cuidado
carpet	la alfombra
carrot	la zanahoria
case	el caso
cat	el gato
to catch a cold	constiparse
Catholic	católico
Catholicism	el catolicismo
cauliflower	la coliflor
cautious	prevenido
certain	cierto
certainty	la certidumbre
chair	la silla
chalk	la tiza
to change	cambiar
chapter	el capítulo
to chat	charlar
cheese	el queso
chef	el cocinero, la cocinera
chess	el ajedrez
chestnut-colored	castaño
chewing gum	el chicle
chicken	el pollo
child	el niño, la niña
Chilean	chileno
Chinese	chino
chocolate	el chocolate
to choke	ahogar, sofocar
chop (pork)	la chuleta
chore	la tarea
Christmas	la Navidad
church	la iglesia
city	la ciudad
class	la clase
to clean	limpiar(se)
clear	claro, transparente
clearly	claramente
client	el cliente
clock	el reloj
to close	cerrar
close by	cerca
clothes	la ropa
cloudy	nublado
cod	el bacalao
coffee	el café
coin	la moneda
cold	frío
college	la escuela universitaria, la universidad
Colombian	colombiano
colon	dos puntos
to come	venir
to come in	entrar
to come to a halt	detenerse
comedian	el cómico
comfortable	cómodo
comma	la coma
to commit suicide	suicidarse
commitment	compromiso
common	común
communist	comunista
community	la comunidad
company	la companía
to complain	quejarse
compromise	el arreglo
computer	la computadora
computing	la informática
to conclude	concluir
condom	el preservativo
to confide	confiar
to conjugate	conjugar
conjunction	la conjunción
to consecrate	consagrar
consequence	la consecuencia
consort	el consorte
constipated (to be)	estar extreñido
contemplation	la contemplación
to continue	continuar, seguir
to contribute to	contribuir a
cook	el cocinero, la cocinera
to cook	cocinar
cookie	la galleta
coppery	cobrizo
corn	el maíz

correct veraz
cosmopolitan el/la cosmopolita
to cost costar, valer
Costa Rican costarricense
costume el vestuario
to count contar
counter-blow el contragolpe
country el país
countryside el campo
cousin el primo, la prima
to cover cubrir, tapar
to cover in plastic enmicar
cover letter la carta de acompañamiento
to crash chocar
cream la crema
crime el delito
croquette la croqueta
to cross atravesar, cruzar
Cuban cubano
culmination la culminación
cup la taza
curly rizado
current actual
curtain la cortina
custard el flan
cute guapo

D

damp húmedo
to dance bailar
dangerous peligroso
Danish danés
to dare to atreverse
dark oscuro
dark brown (eyes) marrón
dark-haired moreno
dash el guión
date (day and month) la fecha
date (appointment) la cita
daughter la hija
daughter-in-law la nuera
day before yesterday anteayer
day el día
dear estimado, querido
December diciembre
deception el engaño
to defend defender
delight el deleite
to demand demandar
Denmark Dinamarca
dentist el/la dentista
denunciation la denuncia
to deny negarse a
to derive from derivar
to descend descender
to deserve merecer
desirable deseable
desk el escritorio
despite a pesar de
despite (as) con todo
to destroy destruir
to devote oneself to dedicarse a
to die morir
diet la dieta
different diferente
difficult difícil
to dignify dignificar
dining room el comedor
dinner la cena
to direct dirigir
disagreement la discordia
disappointment la decepción
discolored decolorado
to discover descubrir
to discuss discutir
to disembark desembarcar
disgrace la deshonra
to do hacer
doctor el médico, la médica
dog el perro
doll la muñeca
Dominican dominicano
Dominican Republic República Dominicana
door la puerta
to doubt dudar
doubtful dudoso
downtown el centro
drawing el dibujo
dress el vestido
to dress vestir
dressed in vestido de
dresser el armario
drink la bebida
to drink beber, tomar
drinking glass el vaso
to drive conducir
to drown ahogar
drums (to play) la batería (tocar)
duchess la duquesa
duck el pato
duet el dúo
during durante
Dutch holandés

E

eagle el águila
early temprano
to earn ganar
easy fácil
to eat comer
Ecuadorian ecuatoriano
educated culto
education la enseñanza
egg el huevo
eggplant la berenjena
Egypt Egipto
Egyptian egipcio
eight hundred ochocientos
eight ocho
eighteen dieciocho
eighth octavo
eighty ochenta
either . . . or o . . . o
electrician el/la electricista
eleven once
e-mail el correo electrónico
embarrassed avergonzado
emotional emocional
employee el empleado
to enchant encantar(le)
to end concluir
end result la culminación
energy la energía
engineer el ingeniero
England Inglaterra
English inglés
to enter entrar
enthusiastic el/la entusiasta
environment el medio ambiente
eraser (board) el borrador
essay el ensayo
to establish establecer
esteemed estimado
even aún
event el suceso
everybody todos
everything todo
example el ejemplo
except excepto, salvo
exclamation mark el signo de exclamación
excuse me con permiso
exercise el ejercicio
exile el exilio
exit la salida
expansive expansivo
to expect imaginarse
expense el gasto

to explain	explicar
to extinguish	extinguir
to extract	extraer
eye	el ojo

F

fabric	la tela
face	la cara
facing	enfrente a, frente a
fact	el dato
factory	la fábrica
fair	justo
faith	la fe
to fall	caer
family	la familia
fan	el aficionado
to fascinate	fascinar(le)
fat	corpulento, gordo
father	el padre
father-in-law	el suegro
February	febrero
to feel	sentir
fever	la fiebre
few	pocos
fiancé	el novio
fiancée	la novia
field	el campo
fifteen	quince
fifth	quinto
fifty	cincuenta
to find one's place	colocarse
to find out	enterar(se)
fine	la multa
finger	el dedo
to finish	acabar, terminar
Finnish	finlandés
to fire	despedir
first	primero
fish (for eating)	el pescado
fish	el pez
to fit	caber
five hundred	quinientos
five	cinco
to fix	arreglar
to flee	huir
floor	el piso
florist's shop	la florería
flower	la flor
fly	la mosca
to fly	volar
folder	la carpeta
to follow	seguir
to forbid	prohibir
to force	obligar a
forearm	el antebrazo
foreigner	el extranjero
foresight	la previsión
forgiveness	el perdón
formation	la formación
former	antiguo
forty	cuarenta
foster	de acogida
four	cuatro
four hundred	cuatrocientos
fourteen	catorce
fourth	cuarto
French	francés
fresh	fresco
Friday	el viernes
friend	el amigo
fritter	el buñuelo
from	desde
fruit	la fruta
full of	lleno de
fun	divertido
funny	gracioso
future	el futuro

G

garden	el jardín
garlic	el ajo
to gather	recoger, reunirse
generally	generalmente
German	alemán
Germany	Alemania
to get	conseguir
to get a job	colocarse
to get angry	enfadarse, enojarse
to get annoyed	molestarse
to get burned	quemarse
to get dressed	vestirse
to get ready	arreglarse
to get together	reunirse
to get up	levantarse
to get used to	acostumbrarse
girl	la chica, la niña
girlfriend	la novia
to give	dar
to give as a gift	regalar
glance	el vistazo
glasses	los anteojos
gloominess	la hosquedad
glove	el guante
to go	ir
to go out	salir
to go to bed	acostarse
to go to sleep	dormirse
goat	el chivo
God	Dios
godfather	el padrino
godmother	la madrina
gold	el oro
good	bueno
gossip	el chisme
to govern	gobernar
to grab	coger, tomar
grade	la nota
grades	la calificación
graduate	licenciado
grammar	la gramática
granddaughter	la nieta
grandfather	el abuelo
grandmother	la abuela
grandson	el nieto
grape	la uva
grapefruit	el pomelo
gray (color)	gris
gray (hair)	canoso
great	gran(de)
Greece	Grecia
Greek	griego
green	verde
greeting	el saludo
to grip	apretar
grocery store	el almacén
to grow	crecer
Guatemalan	guatemalteco
guest	el invitado
to guide	guiar
gym	el gimnasio

H

hair	el cabello, el pelo
haircut	corte de pelo
Haitian	haitiano
half	medio
ham	el jamón
hand	la mano
handkerchief	el pañuelo
to happen	pasar
happiness	la alegría
happy	feliz
hardworking	trabajador
hat	el sombrero
to have	tener
to have fun	divertirse
to have lunch	almorzar
hazel	color de avellana
healthy	sano
to hear	oír
heat	el calor
heel	el tacón

height la estatura
hello hola
to help ayudar
help-wanted ad el anuncio de empleo
here aquí
herself ella misma
hierarchy la jerarquía
high alto
high school la secundaria, el liceo
himself mismo
history la historia
hobby la diversión
home la casa
home page la página principal
homework las tareas
homicide el homicidio
Honduran hondureño
to hope esperar
hot caliente
hour la hora
house la casa
how much/many? cuánto
how? cómo
hug el abrazo
humid húmedo
hundred cien
Hungarian húngaro
Hungary Hungría
hunger la hambre
to hurry apresurarse a
to hurt doler, lastimar
husband el marido, el esposo
hyphen el guión

I

ice cream el helado
idiom el modismo
if si
illiterate analfabeto
in agreement de acuerdo
in case en caso de que
in front of delante de
in order that a fin de que
inaction la inacción
to include incluir
to increase aumentar
incredible increíble
Indian hindú
to influence influenciar
information la información
insecticide el insecticida
inside adentro, dentro de
interactive interactivo
to interest interesar
interested interesado
interesting interesante
interjection la interjección
international internacional
interview la entrevista
to invite to invitar a
Iranian iraní
Iraqi iraquí
Ireland Irlanda
Irish irlandés
Israeli israelí
Italian italiano
itself mismo

J

jacket la chaqueta
January enero
Japan el Japón
Japanese japonés
jewelry las joyas
Jewish judío
job el empleo
to join reunir
joke el chiste
joy la alegría
Judaism el judaísmo
juice el jugo
juicy jugoso
July julio
to jump saltar, tirarse
June junio
just justo, simple
justice el juicio

K

key el botón
key la llave
killer el matón
kitchen la cocina
kitchenette la cocineta
knee la rodilla
to know conocer, saber
Korea Corea
Korean coreano

L

to lack faltar(le)
lamb el cordero
language el idioma
large gran(de)
last name el apellido
last último
late tarde
lately últimamente
latitude la latitud
to laugh reír
Laundromat la lavandería
lawn el césped
lawyer el abogado, la abogada
lazy holgazán
leader el líder
leadership el liderazgo
leaf la hoja
to learn aprender
to leave quedar, salir
Lebanese libanés
Lebanon Líbano
lecture la charla, la conferencia
left izquierdo
leg la pierna
legumes las legumbres
to lend prestar
lentil la lenteja
less menos
lesson la lección
letter la carta
lettuce la lechuga
level el nivel
liberty la libertad
librarian el bibliotecario, la bibliotecaria
library la biblioteca
to lie mentir
light la luz
to light encender
like that así
like como
to like gustar(le)
to link enlazar
lips los labios
to listen escuchar
to live vivir
liver el hígado
livingroom la sala
to load cargar
lobster la langosta
long largo
look la mirada, el vistazo
to look for buscar
to lose perder
lottery la lotería
love el amor
lovely bello, lindo
loyalty la lealdad
luck la suerte
lullaby la canción de cuna

M

magazine la revista
mailbox el buzón

to make hacer
man el hombre
manageable controlable, manejable
manager el/la gerente
many muchos
map el mapa
marathon el maratón
March marzo
market el mercado
to marry (each other) casar(se)
math las matemáticas
matter el asunto, la cuestión
mattress el colchón
May mayo
maybe quizá, quizás, tal vez
to mean significar
to measure medir
to measure out (dose) dosificar
meat la carne
medium mediano
to mention mencionar
menu la carta, el menú
mercy la merced, la misericordia, la piedad
Mexican mexicano
microwave el microondas
midday mediodía
midnight medianoche
milk la leche
milk shake el batido
million el millón
millionaire el millonario
miniskirt la minifalda
misfortune la desgracia
Miss señorita, Srta.
mistake el error
to moan gemir
modern moderno
monarchy la monarquía
Monday el lunes
money el dinero, la plata
more más
morning la mañana
Moroccan marroquí
Morocco Marruecos
mother la madre
mother-in-law la suegra
motorcycle la motocicleta
mountain la montaña
mouse el ratón
moustache el bigote
mouth la boca
to move conmover
to move, change residence mudar(se)
to move something closer acercar
movie la película
movies el cine
moving emocionante
Mr. señor, Sr.
Mrs., Ms. señora, Sra.
mushroom el champiñón
music la música
mussel el mejillón
must deber
myself mismo, misma

N

name el nombre
to name llamar
nap la siesta
nationality la nacionalidad
near cerca de
necklace el collar
to need necesitar
neither, either tampoco
neither . . . nor ni . . . ni
nephew el sobrino
network la red
never jamás, nunca
never once ninguna vez
nevertheless sin embargo
New York Nueva York
New Yorker neoyorquino
New Zealand Nueva Zelanda
New Zealander neocelandés
new nuevo
news las noticias
next próximo
next to al lado de
Nicaraguan nicaragüense
nice amable, lindo, simpático
niece la sobrina
night la noche
nine nueve
nine hundred novecientos
nineteen diecinueve
ninety noventa
ninth noveno
no one nadie
noise el ruido
none ninguno
nonfiction la literatura no novelesca
Norway Noruega
Norwegian noruego
note la nota
notebook el cuaderno
nothing nada
nothing but puro
noun el sustantivo
November noviembre
nurse la enfermera, el enfermero

O

to obey obedecer
obligation el compromiso
obviously obviamente
October octubre
to offer ofrecer
office la oficina
offline fuera de línea
often a menudo, muchas veces
oil el aceite
old viejo
old age la vejez
older mayor
olive la aceituna
on (top of) sobre
on time a tiempo
once alguna vez
one to one unívoco
one uno
onion la cebolla
online en línea
only sólo
open abierto
to open abrir
opinion la opinión
optimistic el/la optimista
orange la naranja
other otro
ourselves mismos, mismas
outside fuera
over encima
to overcome vencer
overcooked recocido
own propio

P

page la hoja, la página
painted pintado de
painter el pintor, la pintora
pair el par, la pareja
Panama el Panamá
Panamanian panameño
pants los pantalones
paper el papel
paradox la paradoja
Paraguayan paraguayo

to paraphrase parafrasear
parasitic parasitario
parents los padres
Parisian parisiense
park el parque
party la fiesta
password la contraseña
pastry el postre
pasture el pasto
patient el paciente
to pay pagar
to pay attention prestar atención
pear la pera
pen el bolígrafo, la pluma
pencil el lápiz
pencil eraser la goma de borrar
people la gente
pepper (condiment) la pimienta
pepper (vegetable) el pimiento
performance (theater) la representación
period el punto
to perjure perjurar
Peruvian peruano
pianist el/la pianista
to pick up levantar
piece el pedazo
piece of information el dato
pier el malecón
pill la pastilla
pillow la almohada
pineapple la piña
pitcher el jarrón
pity la lástima, la pena
place el lugar
plane el avión
planet el planeta
to plant plantar
play la obra
to play jugar, tocar
to play the drums tocar la batería
player el jugador
please por favor
poetess la poetisa
poetry la poesía
Poland Polonia
Polish polaco
polite educado
politics la política
poor pobre
pork la carne de cerdo
Portuguese portugués
possibly posiblemente
poster el cartel
potatoes las papas
poultry la ave
precisely precisamente
precooked precocinado
to prefer preferir
prefix el prefijo
pregnancy el embarazo
to prepare to prepararse a
preposition la preposición
present (gift) el regalo
present el presente
presentation la presentación
preservative el conservador
president el presidente, la presidenta
to pretend fingir
pretext el pretexto
pretty bonito, lindo
printer la impresora
prize el premio
probably probablemente
problem el problema
to proclaim proclamar
to produce producir
professor el catedrático
prologue el prólogo
pronoun el pronombre
to propel propulsar
to propose proponer
to protect proteger
provided that con tal de que
public público
Puerto Rican puertorriqueño
pure puro
purity la pureza
to put colocar, poner
to put a lid on tapar
to put on makeup maquillarse
to put to bed acostar
to put up with soportar

Q

question mark el signo de interrogación
question la cuestión
quiet la quietud
quiz la prueba
quotation marks las comillas

R

rabbit el conejo
to rain llover
rain la lluvia
to raise levantar
rare excepcional, poco común, raro
raspberry la frambuesa
rather bastante, más bien
to read leer
reader el lector, la lectora
reading la lectura
ready listo
real verdadero
to realize darse cuenta
really efectivamente, verdaderamente
reason la razón
recommendation la recomendación
to reconsider recapacitar
to record grabar
red rojo
red (hair) pelirrojo
reddish rojizo
to re-elect reeligir
to refill recargar
to refuse negarse a, rechazar
regardless no obstante
relatives los parientes
relevance la pertinencia
religion la religión
to remain permanecer
to remember acordarse recordar
to remove quitar(se)
to repeat repetir
to resemble parecerse
rest descansar
(the) rest los demás
restaurant el restaurante
resume el curriculum profesional
to return regresar, volver
rice and beans el arroz con frijoles
rice pudding el arroz con leche
rich rico
riches la riqueza
right (direction) derecho
to ring sonar
river el río
road el camino
roof el techo
room el cuarto
rope la cuerda
royal real

to run correr
Russian ruso

S

sad triste
sadness la tristeza
saint el santo, la santa
salad la ensalada
salary el sueldo
salt la sal
Salvadoran salvadoreño
same mismo
sane cuerdo
Saturday el sábado
sauce la salsa
sausage el chorizo, la salchicha
to say decir
to say goodbye despedirse
scar la cicatriz
scarcely apenas
scarf la bufanda
schedule el horario
scholarly escolástico
school la escuela
Scotland Escocia
Scottish escocés
sea el mar
seafront el malecón
seafood los mariscos
second segundo
second to last penúltimo
secret el secreto
to see ver
to seem parecer
self-defense la autodefensa
to sell vender
semicolon el punto y coma
to send enviar, mandar
sensible razonable, sensato
sensitive sensible
September septiembre
to serve atender, servir
to settle arreglar
seven siete
seven hundred setecientos
seventeen diecisiete
seventh séptimo
seventy setenta
to sew coser
shame la vergüenza
to shave afeitar(se)
to shine lucir
shiny brillante
shirt la camisa
shoe el zapato
shoe store la zapatería
shop la tienda
short bajo, corto
to show mostrar
shower la ducha
shrimp el camarón, la gamba, el langostino
to shrink encoger
to shut up callarse
sick enfermo
sick of harto de
side el lado
signature la firma
silver la plata
similarity la semejanza
simple simple
simplicity la simplicidad
since desde
sincere sincero
sincerely atentamente
to sing cantar
sister la hermana
to sit sentarse
site el sitio
six seis
six hundred seiscientos
sixteen dieciséis
sixth sexto
sixty sesenta
size el tamaño
to ski esquiar
skill la habilidad
sky el cielo
slash (/) la barra
to sleep dormir
slowly despacio
small pequeño
to smell oler
smile la sonrisa
to smoke fumar
snake la serpiente
sneaker la zapatilla de deportes
to snow nevar
so much tanto
so that de manera que, para que
so así
soap el jabón
soccer el fútbol
socks las medias
sofa el sofá
solitude la soledad
solution la solución
some algún, cierto
somebody alguien
someone alguien
something algo
sometime alguna vez
sometimes a veces, algunas veces
son el hijo
song la canción
son-in-law el yerno
soon pronto
soup (bouillon) el caldo
soup la sopa
Spain España
Spanish (Castilian) language castellano
Spanish (from Spain) español
to speak hablar
species la especie
to spell deletrear
spinach la espinaca
spouse el esposo, la esposa
to spy espiar
squid el calamar
stain la mancha
star la estrella
to start again recomenzar
to start to echarse a, ponerse a
steak (beef) el bistec
still todavía
to stop parar, detener
story la historia
stoutness la corpulencia
straight (hair) liso
straight derecho
strange extraño
strange raro
straw la paja
strawberry la fresa
street la calle
to stroll pasear
strong fuerte
student el/la estudiante
study el estudio
to study aprender, estudiar
stuffed peppers los chiles rellenos
stupendously estupendamente
subjunctive subjuntivo
to sublet subarrendar
to substitute sustituir
to succeed in llegar a

success el éxito
Sudanese sudanés
suffix el sufijo
to suffocate sofocar
sugar el azúcar
suicide el suicidio
suit el traje
to suit convenir(le)
summer el verano
sun el sol
Sunday el domingo
superfine extrafino
to support mantener, apoyar
surface la superficie
to survive pervivir
Sweden Suecia
Swedish sueco
to swim nadar
Swiss suizo
Switzerland la Suiza
to sympathize with compadecer

T

table la mesa
Taiwanese taiwanés
to take tomar
to take a bath bañarse
take off quitar(se)
talented talentoso
tall alto
to teach how to enseñar a
teacher, elementary el maestro, la maestra
teacher, high school el profesor, la profesora
team el equipo
teaspoon la cucharita
telephone (number) el teléfono
television la televisión
to tell contar
ten diez
tent (camping) la tienda de campaña
tenth décimo
term el término
test el examen
Thai tailandés
Thailand Tailandia
to thank agradecer
that one aquél, ése
that aquel, ese
that que, quien
theater el teatro
themselves mismos, mismas
there donde
thesis la tesis
thief el ladrón, la ladrona
thin delgado, flaco
to think pensar
third tercero
thirteen trece
thirty treinta
this este
this one éste
thought el pensamiento
thousand mil
three tres
three hundred trescientos
thrilling emocionante
to throw tirar, botar
Thursday el jueves
ticket el boleto
time el tiempo, la vez
tired cansado
to the side of al lado de
today hoy
together juntos
tolerance la tolerancia
tomato el tomate
tomorrow mañana
too, also también
too (adverb modifying adjective) demasiado
tool la herramienta
tooth el diente
top la capa
to touch tocar
to touch (emotionally) comover
town el pueblo
toy el juguete
traffic el tráfico
train el tren
training la formación
traitor el traicionero
to translate traducir
translation la traducción
trash la basura
to travel viajar
tree el árbol
trillion el billón
truck el camión
true cierto
to trust fiarse de
truth la verdad
to try pretender
Tuesday el martes
tuna el atún
turkey el pavo
Turkey Turquía
Turkish turco
twelve doce
twenty veinte
twin el gemelo, el mellizo
two dos
two hundred doscientos
typical típico

U

ugly feo
ultimately al final
umbrella el paraguas
uncle el tío
under debajo
underemployment el subempleo
to undo desabrochar
uneducated analfabeto
uniform el uniforme
unique único
United Kingdom Reino Unido
United States los Estados Unidos
united unido
university la universidad
unless a menos que
unlucky pobre
unnatural antinatural
until hasta
Uruguayan uruguayo
useful útil
useless inútil

V

various diferentes, varios
to vary variar
vase el jarrón
veal la ternera
vegetables (green) los vegetales
vegetables las legumbres
Venezuelan venezolano
vengeance la venganza
verb el verbo
very muy
Vietnamese vietnamita
vinegar el vinagre
violence la violencia

W

wages (often hourly) el salario
waiter el camarero
waitress la camarera
to walk andar, caminar
to walk (a dog) pasear

wall	la pared
to want	querer
war	la guerra
to wash	lavar(se)
wastebasket	la cesta
watch	el reloj
water	el agua
to water	regar
way	el camino
wealth	la riqueza
weather	el tiempo
Web page	la página Web
wedding	la boda
Wednesday	el miércoles
week	la semana
weekend	el fin de semana
welcome	bienvenidos
well	bien
well-mannered	educado
what	qué
when	cuándo, cuando
where	dónde, donde
which	cuál, cual
whichever	cualquier, cualquiera
while	mientras
white	blanco
who	quién, quien
whoever	quienquiera
why	por qué
wife	la esposa, la mujer
will	la voluntad
to wilt	marchitar(se)
to win	ganar, vencer
wind	el viento
wisdom	la sabiduría
wise	sabio
wise person	el sabio
with	con
with me	conmigo
with you	contigo
to wither	marchitar(se)
without a doubt	sin duda
without	sin (que)
woman	la mujer
wonderful	maravilloso
work	la obra, el trabajo
to work	trabajar
worker	el obrero, trabajador
world	el mundo
worse	peor
worst	el peor
to write	escribir
writing	la escritura
wrong	equivocado

Y

yard	el jardín
year	el año
yes	sí
yesterday	ayer
young	joven
younger	menor
yourself	mismo, misma
yourselves	mismos, mismas
youth	el/la joven

Z

zero	cero

APPENDIX C

Spanish to English Glossary

A

la abeja	bee
abierto	open
el abogado, la abogada	lawyer
el abrazo	hug
abril	April
abrir	to open
la abuela	grandmother
el abuelo	grandfather
aburrido	boring, bored
aburrir	to bore
aburrirse	to be bored
acá	around here
acabar	to finish
el aceite	oil
la aceituna	olive
acercar	to move something closer
acercarse	to approach
aconsejar	to advise
acordarse	to remember
acostar	to put to bed
acostarse	to go to bed
acostumbrarse	to get used to
la actitud	attitude
la actriz	actress
actual	current
actualmente	at present
actuar	to act
el acusador	accuser
adentro	inside
el adjetivo	adjective
adónde	to where
el adverbio	adverb
afeitar(se)	to shave
el aficionado	fan
a fin de que	in order that
afligir	to afflict
agosto	August
agradecer	to thank
el agua	water
el aguacate	avocado
el águila	the eagle
ahogar	to choke, to drown
el ajedrez	chess
el ajo	garlic
alegrarse	to be happy
la alegría	joy, happiness
alemán	German
Alemania	Germany
al final	ultimately
la alfombra	carpet
algo	something
alguien	someone, somebody
algún	some
algunas veces	sometimes
alguna vez	once, sometime
al ajillo	in garlic sauce
al horno	baked
al lado de	next to, to the side of
el almacén	grocery store
la almohada	pillow
almorzar	to have lunch
alrededor	around
alto	high, tall
amable	nice
ambos, ambas	both
a menos que	unless
a menudo	often
el amigo	friend
el amor	love
analfabeto	illiterate, uneducated
la anarquía	anarchy
andar	to walk
anteayer	day before yesterday
el antebrazo	forearm
antemano	beforehand
los anteojos	glasses
antes	before
antiguo	former, ancient
antinatural	unnatural
la antipatía	antipathy
el antisudoral	antiperspirant
el antojito	appetizer
anunciar	to announce
el anuncio de trabajo	help-wanted ad
el año	year
aparecer	to appear
el apartamento	apartment
el apellido	last name
apenas	scarcely
a pesar de	despite
el apetito	appetite
el aplauso	applause
aprender	to learn, to study
el aprendizaje	apprenticeship
apresurarse a	to hurry
apretar	to grip
aquél	that one
aquel	that
aquí	here
a quien corresponda	to whom it may concern
el árbol	tree
la arepa	corn pancake
Argelia	Algeria
argelino	Algerian
argentino	Argentinean

el armario dresser
arreglar to fix, settle, arrange
arreglarse to get ready
el arreglo compromise
el arroz con frijoles rice and beans
el arroz con leche rice pudding
así like that, so
asistir to attend
el asunto matter
el ateísmo atheism
la atención attention
atender to serve
atentamente sincerely
atento attentive, sincere
a tiempo on time
atravesar to cross
atreverse to dare to
atribuir to attribute
el atún tuna
aumentar to increase
aún even
aunque although
australiano Australian
austríaco Austrian
la autobiografía autobiography
el autobús bus
la autodefensa self-defense
el autor author
la autorización authorization
la avaricia avarice
la ave poultry
a veces sometimes
avergonzado embarrassed
el avión plane
ayer yesterday
ayudar to help
el azúcar sugar
azul blue

B

el bacalao cod
bailar to dance
bajo short
el bancario banker
el banco bank, bench
bañar to bathe
bañarse to take a bath
la barra / (slash)
bastante rather
la basura trash
la batería (tocar) drums (to play)
el batido milk shake
el bebé baby
beber to drink
la bebida drink
belga Belgian
Bélgica Belgium
bello beautiful, lovely
la berenjena eggplant
la biblioteca library
el bibliotecario librarian
bien well
bienvenidos welcome
el bigote moustache
el billón trillion
el bistec (beef) steak
blanco white
la boca mouth
la boda wedding
el boleto ticket
el bolígrafo pen
boliviano Bolivian
bonito pretty
el borrador board eraser
el bote boat
el botón key
el Brasil Brazil
brasileño Brazilian
brillante shiny
bueno good
la bufanda scarf
el buñuelo fritter
buscar to look for
el buzón mailbox

C

el cabello hair
caber to fit
cada each
caer to fall
café brown
el café coffee
la caja box
el calamar squid, calamari
el caldo clear soup
caliente hot
la calificación grades
callarse to be quiet, to shut up
la calle street
el calor heat
la cama bed
la camarera waitress
el camarero waiter
el camarón shrimp
cambiar to change
caminar to walk
el camino road, way
el camión truck
la camiseta shirt
el campamento camp
el campanario bell tower
el campo field, countryside
el Canadá Canada
canadiense Canadian
la canción song
la canción de cuna lullaby
cansado tired
cantar to sing
la capa top
el capítulo chapter
el capricho caprice
la cara face
cargar to load
cariñoso affectionate
la carne meat
la carne de cerdo pork
la carne de res beef
la carpeta folder
la carta menu, letter
la carta de acompañamiento cover letter
el cartel poster
la casa house, home
casar(se) to marry (each other)
casi almost
el caso case
castaño chestnut-colored
castellano Spanish language
el catedrático professor
el catolicismo Catholicism
católico Catholic
catorce fourteen
la cebolla onion
la cena dinner
el centro downtown
cepillar(se) to brush (teeth, hair)
cerca (de) close by, near
cero zero
cerrar to close
la certidumbre certainty
el césped lawn
la cesta wastebasket
el ceviche fish or seafood cured in lemon juice
el champiñón mushroom
la chaqueta jacket
la charla lecture
charlar to chat

la chica girl
el chicle chewing gum
el chico boy
chileno Chilean
los chiles rellenos stuffed peppers
chino Chinese
el chisme gossip
el chiste joke
el chivo goat
chocar to crash
el chocolate chocolate
el chorizo pork sausage
la chuleta (pork) chop
la cicatriz scar
el cielo sky
cien hundred
cierto some, true, certain
cinco five
cincuenta fifty
el cine movies
la cita date
la ciudad city
claramente clearly
claro bright, clear
la clase class
el cliente client
cobrizo coppery
el coche car
la cocina kitchen
cocinar to cook
el cocinero, la cocinera cook, chef
la cocineta kitchenette
coger to grab
el colchón mattress
el colegio high school
el coliflor cauliflower
el collar necklace
colocar to put
colocarse to get a job, to find one's place
colombiano Colombian
color de avellana hazel
la coma comma
el comedor dining room
comenzar a to begin to
comer to eat
el cómico comedian
las comillas quotation marks
cómo how?
como as, like
cómodo comfortable
compadecer to sympathize with
la compañía company
comportarse bien to be well behaved
comprar to buy
compromiso obligation, commitment
la computadora computer
común common
la comunidad community
comunista communist
con with
concluir to end, to conclude
conducir to drive
el conejo rabbit
la conferencia lecture
confiar to confide
la conjunción conjunction
conjugar to conjugate
conmigo with me
conmover to move, to touch
conocer to know
con permiso excuse me
consagrar to consecrate
la consecuencia consequence
conseguir to get, to achieve
el conservador preservative
el consorte consort, accomplice
constiparse to catch a cold
con tal de que provided that
contar to tell, to count
la contemplación contemplation
contestar to answer
contigo with you
continuar to continue
con todo despite, as
contra against
la contracubierta back cover
el contragolpe counter-blow
contrapelo against the grain
la contraseña password
contribuir a to contribute to
convenir(le) to suit
el cordero lamb
Corea Korea
coreano Korean
la corpulencia stoutness
corpulento fat
el correo electrónico e-mail
correr to run
corte de pelo haircut
la cortina curtain
corto short
coser to sew
el/la cosmopolita cosmopolitan
costar to cost
costarricense Costa Rican
crecer to grow
creer to believe
la crema cream
la croqueta croquette
cruzar to cross
el cuaderno notebook
cuál which?
cual which
cualquier whichever
cuándo when?
cuando when, then
cuánto how much/many?
cuanto as much/many
cuarenta forty
cuarto fourth
el cuarto room, bedroom
cuatro four
cuatrocientos four hundred
cubano Cuban
cubrir to cover
la cucharita teaspoon
la cuenta bill
la cuerda rope
cuerdo sane
el cuerpo body
la cuestión matter, question
el cuidado care
la culminación culmination, end result
culto educated
el cumpleaños birthday
el curriculum profesional resume

D

danés Danish
dar to give
darse cuenta to realize
el dato fact, piece of information
de acogida foster
de acuerdo in agreement
debajo under
deber must
la decepción disappointment
décimo tenth
decir to say
decolorado discolored
dedicarse a to devote oneself to
el dedo finger
defender to defend
delante de in front of
el deleite delight

deletrear	to spell
delgado	thin
el delito	crime
demandar	to demand
de manera que	so that
demasiado	too (adverb modifying an adjective)
demás	the rest
el/la dentista	dentist
dentro de	inside
la denuncia	denunciation
derecho	straight, right
derivar	to derive from
desabrochar	to undo
el desayuno	breakfast
descansar	rest
descender	to descend
descubrir	to discover
desde	from, since
deseable	desirable
desembarcar	to disembark
la desgracia	misfortune
la deshonra	disgrace
despacio	slowly
despedir	to fire
despedirse	to say goodbye
después de	after
destruir	to destroy
detener	to bring to a halt
detrás	behind
detenerse	to come to a halt
el día	day
el dibujo	drawing
diciembre	December
el diente	tooth
diez	ten
diecinueve	nineteen
dieciocho	eighteen
dieciséis	sixteen
diecisiete	seventeen
la dieta	diet
diferente	different
difícil	difficult
dignificar	to dignify
Dinamarca	Denmark
el dinero	money
Dios	God
la dirección	address
dirigir	to direct
la discordia	disagreement
discutir	to discuss
la diversión	fun, a hobby
divertido	fun
divertirse	to have fun

doce	twelve
doler	to hurt
el domingo	Sunday
dominicano	Dominican
dónde	where?
donde	where, there
dormir	to sleep
dormirse	to go to sleep
dos	two
doscientos	two hundred
dosificar	to measure out (dose)
dos puntos	colon
la ducha	shower
dudar	to doubt
dudoso	doubtful
el dulce	candy, sweet
el dúo	duet
la duquesa	duchess
durante	during

E

echarse a	to start to
ecuatoriano	Ecuadorian
el edificio	building
educado	well-mannered, polite
efectivamente	really
egipcio	Egyptian
Egipto	Egypt
el ejemplo	example
el ejercicio	exercise
el/la electricista	electrician
el embarazo	pregnancy
emocional	emotional
emocionante	thrilling, moving
la empanada	savory stuffed pastry, usually with meat
empezar (a)	to begin (to)
el empleado	employee
el empleo	job
encantar(le)	to enchant, delight
en caso de que	in case
encender	to light
encima	over
encoger	to shrink
en cuanto	as soon as
la energía	energy
enero	January
enfadarse	to get angry
la enfermera	nurse
enfermo	sick
enfrente a	facing, across from
el engaño	deception
el ingeniero	engineer
enlazar	to link
en línea	online

enmicar	to cover in plastic
enojarse	to get angry
la ensalada	salad
el ensayo	essay
la enseñanza	education
enseñar a	to teach how to
enterar(se)	to find out
entrar	to come in, to enter
entre	between
la entrevista	interview
el/la entusiasta	enthusiastic
enviar	to send
el equipo	team
equivocado	wrong
el error	mistake
escocés	Scottish
Escocia	Scotland
escolástico	academic, scholarly
escribir	to write
el escritorio	desk
la escritura	writing
escuchar	to listen
la escuela	school
la escuela universitaria	college
ése	that one
ese	that
España	Spain
español	Spanish (from Spain)
la especie	species
esperar	to hope
espiar	to spy
la espinaca	spinach
la esposa	wife, spouse
el esposo	husband, spouse
esquiar	to ski
establecer	to establish
los Estados Unidos	United States
estadounidense	American
el estante	bookshelf
estar	to be (located)
estar extreñido	to be constipated
estatura	height
éste	this one
este	this
estimado	dear, esteemed
la estrella	star
el/la estudiante	student
estudiar	to study
el estudio	study
estupendamente	stupendously
el examen	test
excepcional	rare
excepto	except

exigir to demand
el exilio exile
el éxito success
expansivo expansive
explicar to explain
extinguir to extinguish
extraer extract, draw
extrafino superfine
el extranjero foreigner, abroad
extraño strange

F

la fábrica factory
fácil easy
faltar(le) to lack
la familia the family
fascinar(le) to fascinate
fastidioso annoying
la fe faith
febrero February
la fecha date
feliz happy
feo ugly
fiarse de to trust
la fiebre fever
la fiesta party
el fin de semana weekend
fingir to pretend
finlandés Finnish
la firma signature
flaco thin
el flan custard
la flor flower
la florería florist's shop
la formación formation, training
la frambuesa raspberry
francés French
frente a facing, across from
la fresa strawberry
fresco fresh
los frijoles beans
frío cold
la fruta fruit
fuera outside
fuera de línea offline
fuerte strong
fumar to smoke
el fútbol soccer
el futuro future

G

la galleta cookie
la gamba large shrimp
ganar to win, earn
el gasto expense
el gato cat
el gemelo twin
gemir to moan
generalmente generally
la gente people
el/la gerente manager
el gimnasio gym
gobernar to govern
la goma de borrar pencil eraser
gordo fat
grabar to record
gracioso funny, amusing
la gramática grammar
gran(de) large, great
Grecia Greece
griego Greek
gris gray
el guante glove
guapo cute
guatemalteco Guatemalan
la guerra war
guiar to guide
el guión dash, hyphen
gustar(le) to like

H

la habilidad ability, skill
hablar to speak
hacer to make, to do
hacerse to become
haitiano Haitian
la hambre hunger
harto de sick of
hasta until
el helado ice cream
la hermana sister
la hermandad brotherhood
el hermano brother
la herramienta tool
el hígado liver
la hija daughter
el hijo son
hindú Indian
la historia history, story
la hoja leaf, page
hola hello
holandés Dutch
holgazán lazy
el hombre man
el homicidio homicide
hondureño Honduran
la hora hour
el horario schedule
la hosquedad gloominess
hoy today
el huevo egg
huir to flee
húmedo humid, damp
húngaro Hungarian
Hungría Hungary

I

el idioma language
la iglesia church
imaginarse to expect
importar(le) to be important
la impresora printer
la inacción inaction
incluir to include
increíble incredible
influir to influence
la información information
la informática computing
Inglaterra England
inglés English
el insecticida insecticide
el intento attempt
interactivo interactive
interesado interested
interesante interesting
interesar to interest
la interjección interjection
internacional international, among nations
inútil useless
el invitado guest
invitar a to invite to
ir to go
iraní Iranian
iraquí Iraqi
Irlanda Ireland
irlandés Irish
israelí Israeli
italiano Italian
izquierdo left

J

el jabón soap
jamás never
el jamón ham
el jamón serrano Spanish cured ham
el Japón Japan
japonés Japanese
el jardín garden
el jarrón vase, pitcher
el jefe boss
la jerarquía hierarchy
joven young
el/la joven youth
las joyas jewelry

el judaísmo Judaism
judío Jewish
el jueves Thursday
el jugador player
jugar to play
el jugo juice
jugoso juicy
el juguete toy
el juicio justice
julio July
junio June
juntos together
justo just, fair

L

los labios lips
el lado side
el ladrón, la ladrona thief
la langosta lobster
el lápiz pencil
largo long
la lástima pity
lastimar to hurt
lastimarse to bother oneself
la latitud latitude
la lavandería Laundromat
lavar(se) to wash
la lealdad loyalty
la lección lesson
la leche milk
la lechuga lettuce
el lector reader
la lectura reading
leer to read
las legumbres vegetables or legume
la lenteja lentil
levantar to raise, pick up
levantarse to wake up, to get up
libanés Lebanese
Líbano Lebanon
la libertad liberty
la librería bookstore
el libro book
el licenciado graduate
el líder leader
el liderazgo leadership
limpiar(se) to clean
lindo nice, lovely
liso straight
listo ready
la literatura no novelesca nonfiction
llamar to call, to name
la llave key
llegar to arrive
llegar a to succeed in
lleno de full of
llover to rain
la llovizna rainfall
lo menos at least
el lomo de cerdo pork loin
la lotería lottery
lucir to shine
el lugar place
el lunes Monday
la luz light

M

la madre mother
madrileño from Madrid
la madrina godmother
los maduros sweet (ripe) fried plantains
el maestro, la maestra elementary school teacher
el maíz corn
mal(o) bad
el malecón pier, seafront
la mancha stain
mandar to send
manejable manageable
la mano hand
mantener to support
la mantequilla butter
la manzana apple
la mañana morning
mañana tomorrow
el mapa map
maquillarse to put on makeup
el maratón marathon
maravilloso wonderful
marchitar(se) to wither, to wilt
el mar sea
el marido husband
los mariscos seafood
marrón dark brown (eyes)
marroquí Moroccan
Marruecos Morocco
el martes Tuesday
marzo March
más more
mas but
más bien rather
las matemáticas math
el matón killer
mayo May
mayor older
mediano medium
medianoche midnight
las medias socks
el médico, la médica doctor
medio half, average
el medio ambiente environment
mediodía midday
medir to measure
el mejillón mussel
mejor best
mencionar to mention
menor younger
menos less
mentir to lie
la mesa table
el mercado market
la merced mercy
merecer to deserve
mexicano Mexican
el microondas microwave
mientras while
el miércoles Wednesday
mil thousand
el millón million
el millonario millionaire
los mil millones billion
la minifalda miniskirt
la mirada look
mismo same, himself, itself
la mochila backpack
moderno modern
el modismo idiom
el mofongo mashed plantains, often with seafood
el mole meat in chile sauce
molestar to annoy, to bother
molestarse to get annoyed
la moneda coin
la montaña mountain
moreno dark brown, dark-haired
morir to die
la mosca fly
mostrar to show
la motocicleta motorcycle
muchas veces often
mucho many, a lot
mudar(se) to move, change residence
la mujer wife, woman
la multa fine
el mundo world
la muñeca doll

la música	music
muy	very

N

nacer	to be born
el nacimiento	birth
la nacionalidad	nationality
nada	nothing
nadar	to swim
nadie	no one
la naranja	orange
la navidad	Christmas
necesitar	to need
negarse a	to deny, to refuse
negro	black
neocelandés	New Zealander
neoyorquino	New Yorker
nevar	to snow
nicaragüense	Nicaraguan
la nieta	granddaughter
el nieto	grandson
ninguna vez	never once
ninguno	none
ni . . . ni	neither . . . nor
la niña	girl, child
el niño	boy, child
el nivel	level
la noche	night
el nombre	name
no obstante	regardless
norteamericano	American
Noruega	Norway
noruego	Norwegian
la nota	note, grade
las noticias	news
novecientos	nine hundred
noveno	ninth
noventa	ninety
la novia	girlfriend, fiancée
noviembre	November
el novio	boyfriend, fiancé
nublado	cloudy
la nuera	daughter-in-law
Nueva York	New York
Nueva Zelanda	New Zealand
nueve	nine
nuevo	new
nunca	never

O

obedecer	to obey
obligar a	to force
la obra	play, work
el obrero	worker
obviamente	obviously
ochenta	eighty
ocho	eight
ochocientos	eight hundred
octavo	eighth
octubre	October
la oficina	office
ofrecer	to offer
oír	to hear
ojalá que	it's hoped that, I hope that
el ojo	eye
oler	to smell
once	eleven
o . . . o	either . . . or
la opinión	opinion
el/la optimista	optimistic
el oro	gold
oscuro	dark
otorgar	to award
otra vez	again
otro	other, another

P

el padre	father
los padres	parents
el padrino	godfather
la paella	a saffron rice dish, usually prepared with seafood
el paciente	patient
pagar	to pay
la página	page
la página Web	Web page
la página principal	home page
el país	country
pajizo	made of straw
el pan	bread
la panadería	bakery
el Panamá	Panama
panameño	Panamanian
los pantalones	pants
el pañuelo	handkerchief
las papas	potatoes
el papel	paper
el par	pair
la paradoja	paradox
parafrasear	to paraphrase
el paraguas	umbrella
paraguayo	Paraguayan
para que	so that
parar	to stop
parasitario	parasitic
pardo	brown
parecer	to seem
parecerse	to resemble
la pared	wall
la pareja	pair
los parientes	relatives
parisiense	Parisian
parpadear	to blink
el parque	park
pasar	to happen
pasear	to stroll, to walk (a dog)
la pastilla	pill
el pasto	pasture
el pato	duck
el pavo	turkey
el pedazo	piece
pedir	to ask
la película	movie
peligroso	dangerous
pelirrojo	red
el pelo	hair
pena	pity
el pensamiento	thought
pensar	to think
penúltimo	second to last
peor	worse, worst
pequeño	small
la pera	pear
perder	to lose
el perdón	forgiveness
perjurar	to perjure
permanecer	to remain
pero	but
el perro	dog
pertenecer	to belong
la pertinencia	relevance
peruano	Peruvian
pervivir	to survive
el pescado	fish
el pez	fish
el/la pianista	pianist
la pierna	leg
la pimienta	pepper (condiment)
el pimiento	pepper (vegetable)
pintado de	painted
el pintor, la pintora	painter
el piso	floor
la piña	pineapple
la pizarra	board
el planeta	planet
plantar	to plant
la plata	silver, money
la playa	beach
la pluma	pen
el pluscuamperfecto	past perfect
pobre	poor, unlucky
poco	a little

poco común	rare
pocos	few
poder	to be able to
la poesía	poetry
la poetisa	poetess
polaco	Polish
la política	politics
el pollo	chicken
Polonia	Poland
el pomelo	grapefruit
poner	to put
ponerse a	to start to
por	by
por favor	please
por qué	why
porque	because
portugués	Portuguese
posiblemente	possibly
el postre	pastry
el pozole	hominy stew
precisamente	precisely
precocinado	precooked
preferir	to prefer
el prefijo	prefix
preguntar	to ask (a question)
el premio	prize
prepararse a	to prepare to
la preposición	preposition
la presentación	presentation
presente	present
el preservativo	condom
el/la presidente	president
prestar	to lend, to pay (attention)
pretender	to try, to hope to achieve
el pretexto	pretext
prevenido	cautious
la previsión	foresight
primero	first
el primo, la prima	cousin
probablemente	probably
el problema	problem
proclamar	to proclaim
producir	to produce
el profesor, la profesora	high school teacher
prohibir	to forbid
el prólogo	prologue
el pronombre	pronoun
pronto	soon
propio	own
proponer	to propose
propulsar	to drive, propel
proteger	to protect
próximo	next
la prueba	quiz
público	public
el pueblo	town
la puerta	door
puertorriqueño	Puerto Rican
el punto	period
el punto y coma	semicolon
la pureza	purity
puro	nothing but, just, pure

Q

qué	what?
que	what, that
quebrar	to break (something)
quebrarse	to break (a bone)
quedar	to leave
quedar(se)	to remain
quejarse	to complain
quemar	to burn
quemarse	to get burned
querer	to want
querido	dear
el queso	cheese
quién	who?
quien	who, that
quienquiera	whoever
la quietud	quiet, calmness
quince	fifteen
quinientos	five hundred
quinto	fifth
quitar(se)	to remove, take off
quizá, quizás	maybe

R

raro	rare, strange
un rato	a while
el ratón	mouse
la razón	reason
razonable	sensible
real	royal
realizar	to actualize
recapacitar	to reconsider
recargar	to refill
recocido	overcooked
recoger	to gather
la recomendación	recommendation
recomenzar	to start again, to recommence
recordar	to remember
rechazar	to refuse
la red	network
reeligir	to re-elect
regalar	to give as a gift
el regalo	present
regar	to water
regresar	to return
Reino Unido	United Kingdom
reír	to laugh
la religión	religion
el reloj	clock, watch
repetir	to repeat
la representación	performance (theater)
la República Dominicana	Dominican Republic
responder	to answer, respond
la respuesta	answer
el restaurante	restaurant
reunir	to join
reunirse	to gather, to get together
la revista	magazine
rico	rich
el río	river
la riqueza	riches, wealth
rizado	curly
la rodilla	knee
rogar	to beg
rojizo	reddish
rojo	red
romance	Romance (language)
romper(se)	to break
la ropa	clothes
rubio	blond
el ruido	noise
ruso	Russian

S

el sábado	Saturday
saber	to know
la sabiduría	wisdom
(el) sabio	wise, a wise person
la sal	salt
la sala	livingroom
el salario	wages (often hourly)
la salchicha	pork sausage
la salida	exit
salir	to go out, to leave
el salpicón	cold non-vegetable salad (usually with seafood)
el saludo	greeting
la salsa	sauce
salvadoreño	Salvadoran
salvo	except
la sangría	a mix of wine and fruit juices
sano	healthy
santo	saint
el secreto	secret
seguir	to follow, to continue

según according to
segundo second
seis six
seiscientos six hundred
sesenta sixty
la semana week
la semejanza similarity
sensato sensible
sensible sensitive
sentar to sit
sentir to feel
señor, Sr. Mr.
señora, Sra. Mrs., Ms.
señorita, Srta. Miss
septiembre September
séptimo seventh
ser to be
la serpiente snake
servir to serve
setecientos seven hundred
setenta seventy
sexto sixth
sí yes
si if
siempre always
la siesta nap
siete seven
significar to mean
el signo de exclamación exclamation mark
el signo de interrogación question mark
la silla chair
simpático nice
simple just, simply, simple
la simplicidad simplicity
sin without
sin duda without a doubt
sin embargo nevertheless
sino but following a negative statement
sin que without
el sitio site
sobre on, on top of
la sobrina niece
el sobrino nephew
el sofá sofa
sofocar to choke, to suffocate
el sol sun
la soledad solitude
sólo only
solo alone
la solución solution, answer
el sombrero hat
sonar to ring
la sonrisa smile
la sopa soup
la sopa de frijoles negros black bean soup
soportar to put up with
sorprenderse to be surprised
subarrendar to sublet
subcutáneo subcutaneous, under the skin
el subempleo underemployment
subjuntivo subjunctive
el suceso event
sudanés Sudanese
Suecia Sweden
sueco Swedish
la suegra mother-in-law
el suegro father-in-law
el sueldo salary
suele does usually (verb)
la suerte luck
el sufijo suffix
suicidarse to commit suicide
el suicidio suicide
la Suiza Switzerland
suizo Swiss
la superficie surface
el sustantivo noun
sustituir to substitute

T

el tacón heel
tailandés Thai
Tailandia Thailand
taiwanés Taiwanese
talentoso talented
tal vez maybe
los tamales corn patties, usually with minced meat
el tamaño size
también too, also
tampoco neither, either
tan . . . como as . . . as
tanto so much
tapar to cover, put a lid on
las tapas appetizer-sized dishes
tarde late
la tarde afternoon
la tarea chore, homework
el/la taxista cab driver
la taza cup
el teatro theater
el techo roof
la tela fabric
el teléfono telephone (number)
la televisión television
temprano early
tener to have
tercero third
terminar to finish
el término term
el ternero calf (animal)
la tesis thesis
la tía aunt
el tiempo time, weather
la tienda shop
la tienda de campaña tent (camping)
el tío uncle
típico typical
tirar to throw
tirarse to jump
la tiza chalk
tocar to touch, to play
tocar la batería to play the drums
el tocino salted pork
todavía still
todo everything, all
todos everybody
la tolerancia tolerance
tomar to take, to drink
el tomate tomato
la torta cake
la tortilla española Spanish potato omelette
los tostones fried plantains
trabajador worker, hardworking
trabajar to work
el trabajo work
la traducción translation
traducir to translate
traer to bring
el tráfico traffic
el traicionero traitor
el traje suit
transparente clear
trece thirteen
treinta thirty
el tren train
tres three
trescientos three hundred
triste sad
la tristeza sadness
turco Turkish
Turquía Turkey
tutearse to address with *tú*

U

último	last
últimamente	lately
único	only, unique
unido	united
el uniforme	uniform
la universidad	college, university
unívoco	one to one
uno	one
uruguayo	Uruguayan
útil	useful
la uva	grape

V

valer	to be worth, to cost
variar	to vary
varios, varias	various
el vaso	drinking glass
los vegetales	green vegetables
veinte	twenty
la vejez	old age
la vela	candle
vencer	to win, to overcome
vender	to sell
venezolano	Venezuelan
la venganza	vengeance
venir	to come
ver	to see
el verano	summer
veraz	correct
el verbo	verb
la verdad	truth
verdaderamente	really
la verdad es que	actually
verdadero	real
verde	green
la vergüenza	shame
el vestido	dress
vestido de	dressed in
vestir	to dress
vestirse	to get dressed
el vestuario	costume
la vez	time
viajar	to travel
viejo	old
el viento	wind
el viernes	Friday
vietnamita	Vietnamese
la violencia	violence
el vistazo	look, glance
el vinagre	vinegar
vivir	to live
volar	to fly
la voluntad	will
volver	to return
vos	you, informal/singular (in parts of Río de la Plata region)

Y

ya	already, now
el yerno	son-in-law
la yucca	a root vegetable similar to a potato

Z

la zanahoria	carrot
la zapatería	shoe store
la zapatilla de deportes	sneaker
el zapato	shoe

Appendix D
Answer Key

Chapter 2

1. Subject: The cars I saw parked outside; predicate: were not very clean.
2. Subject: I; predicate: wanted to buy a jacket that would fit me well.
3. Subject: Students and their parents; predicate: eagerly waited their turn.
4. Subject: It; predicate: rained frequently.
5. Subject: Everybody in the audience; predicate: clapped.

1. interesting–adjective
2. huh–interjection
3. made–verb
4. humor–noun
5. to blame–verb

Chapter 3

1. cantábamos
2. difícil
3. camarones
4. recomendación
5. póntelo
6. voluntad

1. 5–cinco
2. 16–dieciséis
3. 27–veintisiete
4. 202–doscientos dos
5. 344–trescientos cuarenta y cuatro
6. 1998–mil novecientos noventa y ocho

1. (4) el cuarto libro
2. (10) la décima historia
3. (1) la primera comunidad
4. (8) el octavo horario

5. (9) el noveno número
6. (7) la séptima página
7. (2) el segundo árbol
8. (6) el sexto dedo

Chapter 4

1. árbol (masculine)
2. dieta (feminine)
3. navidad (feminine)
4. malecón (masculine)
5. solución (feminine)
6. tienda (feminine)
7. problema (masculine)
8. paraguas (masculine)
9. ajedrez (masculine)
10. especie (feminine)

1. la consecuencia–las consecuencias
2. el microondas–los microondas
3. un pez–unos peces
4. una cocina–unas cocinas
5. el ratón–los ratones
6. un matador–unos matadores
7. la merced–las mercedes
8. un café–unos cafés

1. Me gusta tomar una siesta <u>los</u> domingos.
2. Escribí <u>unos</u> poemas para ella.
3. Me duele <u>la</u> cabeza.
4. Mi papá es abogado. (no article)
5. Tengo <u>un</u> regalo para ti.
6. Ya pasaron <u>unas</u> semanas desde que te vi por <u>la</u> última vez.
7. <u>Los</u> Sánchez me invitaronn a su casa a cenar con (no article) ellos.
8. ¡Qué bebé más dulce! (no article)

1. Maria's house–la casa de Maria
2. Ricardo's brother's wife–la esposa del hermano de Ricardo
3. the class teacher–la profesora de clase
4. the doctor's patients–los pacientes del doctor (or: los pacientes de la doctora)
5. the children's toys–los juguetes de los niños
6. today's lesson–la lección de hoy

Chapter 5

1. the boys–ellos
2. you (informal) and I–tú y yo, nosotros
3. you (formal) and I–usted y yo, nosotros
4. Elena, Marta, Diana, y Martín–ellos

5. two of you (informal)–vosotros
6. el primo–él

1. el profesor de matemáticas–usted
2. tus amigos–vosotros (in Spain), ustedes (everywhere else)
3. tu hermana menor–tú
4. tus abuelos–ustedes
5. una mujer en la calle–usted
6. los lectores de tu escritura–vosotros or ustedes, depending on context

1. Tú la compraste.
2. Ellos los están buscando.
3. Los veo desde la vantana.
4. Ella nos encontró en el bar.

1. El doctor le tapó a Mariano las rodillas.
2. Nuestra tía nos regaló a nosotros muchos juguetes.
3. Nosotros les decimos a ustedes la verdad.
4. Mi mamá me dijo a mí que debo estudiar muy bien.

1. Los llaves de Elena son sus llaves.
2. El coche mío es mi coche.
3. Los estudios de nosotros son nuestros estudios.
4. El cuarto tuyo es tu cuarto.
5. El dibujo de Mario es su dibujo.
6. Los proyectos de Antonio y Selena son sus proyectos.

Chapter 6

1. las naranjas jugosas
2. los libros interesantes
3. la chica bonita
4. las estrellas brillantes
5. la ropa cómoda
6. el café caliente

1. bueno + idea: la buena idea
2. interesante + cuento: el cuento interesante
3. equivocado + opinión: la equivocada opinión/la opinión equivocada (depending on context)
4. pequeño + perritos: los pequeños perritos
5. tercero + intento: el tercer intento
6. rojo + bufandas: las bufandas rojas

1. Dirk es de Alemania. Es alemán.
2. Fabrizio y Kachina son del Brasil. Son brasileños.
3. Patrick es del Canadá. Es canadiense.
4. María es de Chile. Es chilena.
5. Daniel y Carlos son de Costa Rica. Son costarricenses.

6. Aziza es de Egipto. Es egipcia.
7. Kathryn y Janet son de los Estados Unidos. Son estadounidenses.
8. Michel es de Francia. Es francés.

1. rápido—rápidamente
2. feliz—felizmente
3. lento—lentamente
4. triste—tristemente
5. atento—atentamente

Chapter 7

1. Ellos hablan (hablar) inglés.
2. Nosotras vivimos (vivir) en Madrid.
3. Usted abre (abrir) la puerta.
4. Vosotros vendéis (vende) frutas en el mercado.
5. Elena prepara (preparar) el desayuno.
6. Ustedes deciden (decidir) que hacer.

1. The professor is arranging his papers.
2. I help my parents with the house chores.
3. We come in from the back door.
4. She cleans her house every week.
5. You need help.
6. They are burning leaves in the yard.

1. Tú bailas bien.
2. Ustedes lavan los platos.
3. Nosotros mandamos cartas a nuestros amigos.
4. Ellos enseñan las clases por las mañanas.
5. Yo bebo mucho agua cada día.
6. Él mira la película.

Chapter 8

1. Los niños juegan (jugar) en su cuarto.
2. Nosotras los vemos (ver) a ellos desde la ventana.
3. ¿Recuerdan (recordar) ustedes lo que deben hacer?
4. Tú cierras (cerrar) el libro.
5. Vosotros queréis (querer) salir a bailar.
6. Ella cuenta (contar) chismes todo el tiempo.
7. Nosotros permanecemos (permanecer) aquí.
8. Yo les exijo (exigir) a mis padres que me dejen salir.
9. Tú mientes (mentir), ¿no es así?
10. Vosotros podéis (poder) descansar un rato.

1. Ella es una ladrona. Es mala.
2. El señor Órtiz es abogado.

3. Mis hijos tienen el pelo negro. Son morenos.
4. Son las once de la noche.
5. Tú tienes fiebre. Estás enfermo.
6. Ustedes son muy simpáticos.
7. Cuando viajamos juntos, yo estoy muy alegre.
8. Yo soy de México. Soy mexicana.
9. No estoy bien. Me siento mal.
10. ¿Está usted alegre hoy?

Chapter 9

1. Caterina sabe la historia de los Estados Unidos.
2. Ellos conocen a todos en la escuela.
3. Nosotros no sabemos qué hacer.
4. ¿Sabes (tú) lo que está pasando afuera?
5. No conozco a ese chico.

1. Ella está leyendo.
2. Hay una caja sobre la mesa.
3. Ellos están caminando.
4. Hablan francés en Francia.
5. ¿Qué tiempo hace?

Chapter 10

1. No tengo dinero. Lo dejé en casa.
2. Me dijeron (a mí) que llegará más tarde.
3. El taxista te llevará (a ti) a casa.
4. Aquí tienes la revista. La puedes leer más tarde.
5. Tengo muchas novelas. Las prefiero a la literatura no novelesca.

1. La enfermera trae las pastillas a nosotros. Nos las trae.
2. Ellos necesitan ayuda. ¿Se la das a ellos?
3. Quieres conducir el coche. Yo te lo presto.
4. Ellos dicen la verdad a vosotros. Ellos vos la dicen.
5. Explico el cuento a Marta y Pedro. Se lo explico.

1. Me gusta bailar.
2. Le encantan los flores.
3. Te quedan cinco dólares.
4. Les falta dinero.
5. Nos interesan tus/vuestros/sus cuentos.

1. Ustedes se cepillan (cepillarse) los dientes dos veces por día.
2. Nosotros nos mudamos (mudarse) a Nueva York el próximo junio.
3. Ramón se afeita (afeitarse) cada mañana.
4. Ellos se enteran (enterarse) de todos mis secretos.
5. Nuestro jefe se viste (vestirse) bien, aún los fines de semana.

Chapter 11

1. ¿(Tú) dormiste (dormir) un rato?
2. Hace tres años que nuestra abuela se murió (morirse).
3. La maestra nunca se cansaba (cansarse) de nuestras preguntas.
4. Generalmente la enfermera comía (comer) el desayuno a las ocho.
5. Yo pensaba (pensar) terminar el trabajo a las cinco, pero terminé (terminar) a las siete.
6. Cuando estábamos (estar) en el grupo de rock, yo toqué (tocar) la guitarra y Ernesto tocó (tocar) la batería.
7. ¿Ya (ella) te dijo (decir) qué pasó?
8. ¿Ustedes leyeron (leer) la novela Rayuela de Julio Cortázar?
9. Los clases acabaron (acabar) en junio.
10. Nosotros dimos (dar) el dinero a la camarera.
11. En aquellos días, ellos preferían (preferir) el cine a los libros.
12. Usted estaba (estar) trabajando cuando se apagó (apagarse) la luz.
13. Los niños estaban (estar) en cama cuando oyeron (oír) los ruidos.
14. Yo conocí (conocer) a mi marido en la fiesta de Navidad.
15. El año pasado, yo dormía (dormir) por lo menos ocho horas cada noche.
16. Ellos vinieron (venir) por la noche.
17. Había (haber) mucha comida para los invitados.
18. El gerente concluyó (concluir) su lectura con aplausos.
19. Yo siempre decía (decir) que no tendrás suerte en este proyecto.
20. Mientras nosotros caminábamos (caminar) a casa, empezó (empezar) a llover.

Chapter 12

1. El armario no cabrá (caber) aquí.
2. Nosotros sabremos (saber) lo que pasó cuando encontremos a María.
3. Habrá (haber) tiempo mañana.
4. Yo tendré (tener) la respuesta el próximo día.
5. Te pondrás (ponerse) tu nuevo traje, ¿verdad?

1. Yo no lo diría (decir) si no fuera la verdad.
2. Si pudiera, ella vendría (venir) hoy.
3. Esto no valdría (valer) la pena.
4. ¿Ustedes querrían (querer) empezar la lectura ya?
5. Nosotros haríamos (hacer) todo si tuviéramos el tiempo.

1. Everyone will come to the party. Everyone is probably coming to the party.
2. I'll come to the restaurant at seven. I'm probably coming to the restaurant at seven.
3. I would do it with you.
4. We would visit our grandparents on Thursday.

Chapter 13

1. Ustedes esperan que la profesora repita (repetir) el trabajo.
2. Él no está seguro que su marido se confíe (confiarse) en ella.

3. Bailamos mientras se toque (tocarse) la música.
4. Tú me aconsejas que yo no piense (pensar) así.
5. Estoy lista en caso de que lleguen (llegar) temprano.
6. Ellos me exigen que yo finja (fingir) alegría.
7. Usted duda que yo me sienta (sentir) bien, ¿verdad?
8. Vosotros necesitáis que yo sea (ser) el médico.
9. Sea (ser) lo que sea (ser).

1. ¡Abre la puerta!
2. ¡No parad!
3. ¡Tome la mano!
4. ¡Vámonos!
5. No comámoslo.

Chapter 14

1. Tú has acabado (acabar) con la cena. You have finished eating dinner.
2. Tú habrás visto (ver) la película antes de la clase mañana. You will have seen the movie before class tomorrow.
3. Vosotros vos habíais levantado (levantar) antes que yo llegué aquí. You had awakened before I got here.
4. Yo habría dicho (decir) la verdad si me hubieran preguntado (preguntar). I would have told the truth if they had asked me.
5. Hemos escrito (escribir) un ensayo juntos. We have written an essay together.
6. No era cierto que tú hubieras ido (ir) por allá. It wasn't certain that you had gone there.
7. Ellos habían terminado (terminar) sus estudios cuando se apagó la luz. They had finished their studies when the lights went off.
8. Todos esperan que yo haya hecho (hacer) el trabajo por mí mismo. Everyone hopes that I have done the job myself.
9. He puesto (poner) la mochila debajo del escritorio. I have put the backpack under the desk.
10. Ellos han sido (ser) estudiantes por muchos años. They have been students for many years.

Chapter 15

1. Me gustaría o jugar el fútbol o nadar en el mar.
2. Él no quiere ni zanahorias ni cebollas en su ensalada.
3. Ellos no quieren ni quedarse en casa ni irse a la playa.
4. Ni él ni ella quieren venir con nosotros.
5. No tengo lápices, sino bolígrafos/plumas.
6. Aunque se siente cansada, se reunirá con el equipo.
7. A pesar de todo lo que está pasando, estamos bien.
8. Sin embargo, ustedes están contentos de estar aquí.

1. Voy a la playa para nadar en el mar.
2. Van al mercado por autobús.
3. Nos gusta pasear por las calles de la ciudad.

4. La cena fue preparada por mí; yo lo preparé.
5. La carpeta con la información está por dentro.
6. Hoy es tu cumpleaños. Este regalo es para ti.
7. He trabajado en la oficina por muchos años.
8. ¿Por qué es así?

Chapter 16

1. Sí, Bogotá es la capital de Colombia.
2. Hoy voy a estudiar español.
3. Soy moreno(a)/soy rubio(a)/soy pelirrojo(a).
4. Porque me gustaría hablar con la gente cuando viaje a México.
5. Abraham Lincoln era presidente durante la Guerra Civil.
6. Este libro es mío.
7. Me gustaría viajar a España con mis amigos.
8. Vivo en Boston.
9. Voy a la Florida.
10. Este libro cuesta $14.95.
11. Tengo una hermana y dos hermanos.
12. Hoy es el 15 de marzo.
13. París es la capital de Francia.
14. En español "*generous*" se dice "generoso."
15. Empecé a estudiar español en el año 1991.

Index

A

B

C

W

Y